WILLIAM FOSSAT

BEFORE I START SINGING

DORRANCE
PUBLISHING CO
EST. 1920
PITTSBURGH, PENNSYLVANIA 15238

Dorrance Publishing Co
585 Alpha Drive
Pittsburgh, PA 15238
Visit our website at *www.dorrancebookstore.com*

ISBN: 978-1-6495-7153-3
eISBN: 978-1-6495-7662-0

And I'll tell it and think it and speak it and breathe it
And reflect from the mountain so all souls can see it
And I'll stand on the ocean until I start sinkin'
But I'll know my song well before I start singin'

—Bob Dylan, "A Hard Rain's A'Gonna Fall"

CONTENTS

Introduction 7
Chapter One: Steinbeck Country 21
Chapter Two: Bad News in Babylon 27
Chapter Three: Three Years to Kill 29
Chapter Four: Cutting the Mustard 31
Chapter Five: Silver Wings 34
Chapter Six: While We're On the Subject 37
Chapter Seven: Cats and Dogs 42
Chapter Eight: Brad Gets the Nod 45
Chapter Nine: A Disease Called Discernment 56
Chapter 10: Higher Than What? 58
Chapter 11: The Ingersoll Watch 60
Chapter 12: A Compelling Argument 63
Chapter 13: The Opiate of the Masses 66
Chapter 14: The One True Church 69
Chapter 15: Matthew, Mark Luke and John 72
Chapter 16: Men Without Women 75
Chapter 17: John the Father 79
Chapter 18: Survival of the Fittest 82
Chapter 19: Hell Week 84
Chapter 20: Snakes and Phallic Symbols 87
Chapter 21: Snakes and City Boys 89
Chapter 22: Exceptions to the Rule 93
Chapter 23: The Other Exception 96
Chapter 24: Everybody But Stu and Me 99
Chapter 25: The Honorable Thing To Do 103
Chapter 26: Bragg Briefs Hits the Fan 105
Chapter 27: Sheep Without A Shepherd 108
Chapter 28: The Champ Versus the Chumps 112
Chapter 29: Regular Programming 115
Chapter 30: Death in the Afternoon 117
Chapter 31: My Mother and My Brethren 121
Chapter 32: My Hat and the Captain's Hat.............. 131

BEFORE I START SINGING

INTRODUCTION

We were first called the Children of God by a newspaper reporter from Camden, New Jersey. The name stuck for a while and we used it. Over the years we were called other names by other reporters—TIME Magazine, in its June, 1972 edition, called us "the storm troopers of the Jesus Revolution"—but amongst ourselves we have always been known simply as "the Family."

In the fifteen countries that I have called home over the years, living under the same roof with other Americans, Japanese, British, Australians, Canadians, Austrians and Germans, Italians, French, Spaniards, New Zealanders, Chinese, Taiwanese, Dutch, Danes and Norwegians, Slovenians, Bosnians and Croats, Serbs, Poles, Ukrainians, Israelis, South Africans, Mexicans; former hippies, former Catholics and Protestants, former Jews and Muslims, former atheists and Communists; men, women and children, cats and dogs; a family is what we have always been to one another.

They said it couldn't be done and warned us not to try. Our friends in the churches told us we were taking the multi-cultural, multi-racial, multi-lingual miracle of first-century Christianity too seriously, that it was never intended by God or the Early Church to become a blueprint for Christian living. To try to resurrect it now, in this modern era, with all of its complexities, would be madness, they said, along with a number of other early Christian doctrines and practices that they said you had to be crazy to believe in, such as scripture memorization, which they called mind control; preaching without a license, which they called disturbing the peace; healing without a license, which they called practicing medicine without a license; getting married without a license, which they called fornicating; educating our children without a license, which they called child abuse.

Among the facts that our early Christian accusers failed to spice their arguments with—some went so far as to call the Early Church "a failed experiment"—was the fact that none of them had ever tried it. Another salient piece of information that never came up in their discourse, or in the court of public opinion, unless we brought it up ourselves, was the patriotic factor. In America, where we had our beginnings, it could fairly be said that allegiance to the flag far overshadowed allegiance to the faith.

Not surprisingly, the guardians of that faith do not like to be reminded of their infidelities, not by us, their children, and especially not in the language of scripture, which sounded a lot different coming out of our mouths than it did from theirs.

My father, for example, was the religious and political spokesman for our family while I was growing up, as well as social commentator, historian, linguist, *raconteur*, disciplinarian, castigator of all unrighteousness. A devout Catholic and an even more devout Republican, he remained adamant, almost until the end, that the God who had brought him and my mother through two World Wars and the Great Depression, two atomic bombs, the Korean War and the Cuban Missile Crisis, establishing his beloved America as the most powerful, most prosperous nation on earth (while establishing my father as vice-president and manager of the second-richest agricultural bank in the State of California); could not afford to not let the Home of the Brave and the Land of the Free fall prey to the whoredoms that had brought every earthly empire to its knees. As He had kept the Children of Israel in their march to the Promised Land, so would He keep America, and bring her, unscathed and undefiled, to her safe haven, her Manifest Destiny.

God was still on the throne in Washington, D. C. if my father had anything to say about it.

November 22nd, 1963, the event that became, for my generation, the keynote address for that decade and the decades that followed, became, for my father's generation (Not my mother's. I daresay that most of the men who hated Kennedy had wives who loved him.), a mere blip on the radar screen of history, a sad but necessary step in the evolution of a young, resilient nation. The war that followed immediately on the heels of the first assassination, followed five years later by the assassination of the president's younger brother, successfully removing the Kennedys from the political landscape, successfully disabled what was left of the American political conscience, if it ever had one.

The rank-and-file, never comfortable with the notion of an enemy within (too close to home, too difficult to define, impossible to prosecute), were quickly given an enemy without, one that they could easily define and easily prosecute, or so they thought at the time. The Vietnamese had other ideas. With their long history of making life miserable for foreign occupiers, they quickly demonstrated to the Americans what they had already demonstrated to the French and the Japanese.

Within a year of the public beheading of the first Catholic president and the demolition of Camelot, before Jackie and John-John and Caroline could get their bags packed and vacate the premises, faster than you can say *coup d'etat*, the intoxicating, liberating smell of gun smoke and burning flesh was back in the air and on the airwaves.

The mothers and fathers of America, after installing LBJ in the White House in the biggest popular landslide since 1820, were given a war that they could watch from their living rooms—with Chet Huntley and David Brinkley—while the deadly fumes that seeped from under the thrones of power in Washington, D. C. went undetected, unreported, and unprosecuted.

The nation would not be saddled with a guilty conscience, not if LBJ had anything to say about it.

While we in the Family were nothing if not a by-product of the American counter-culture, which included the hippies, the weed-smoking, acid-dropping, bed-hopping, flesh-flaunting anarchists who drove our parents up the wall; the equally disreputable anti-war element and the black power movement, along with the Jewish-led political factions that helped to define what American youth would should be for and against; before any of this we were the children of the affluent, sons and daughters of well-to-do Christian and Jewish families, programmed to become nothing that our parents did not want us to become, which did not include our becoming Jesus freaks.

We were the college-prep generation, high-schoolers chosen by President Kennedy to lead the charge against the Russians. Remember the Russians? In those days they were called the Soviet Union, or "the Soviets." In the 15 years since the Great Patriotic War, as they called it, in which an estimated 27 *million* of her citizens perished in the fight against Hitler, compared with less than half a million Americans, breaking the back of the German army before the Americans ever fired a shot, Mother Russia had not only resurrected her military and become a nuclear superpower, she led the world in science and space technology, in the arts (ballet, classical music, literature), in amateur athletics (gymnastics, boxing, wrestling, weightlifting).

Whatever else she had become in the eyes of her former allies in the West, her performance on the world stage had made her a persistent embarrassment to the American public school system, which was cranking out 18-year-olds who could barely read or write or speak the mother tongue.

Heirs of the American Dream, my generation was exhorted by the President to rise above the complacency and the mediocrity of the postwar years, to carry our dreams and our freedoms to the citizens of other nations, to those less fortunate than ourselves. The Peace Corps was born. These heady, hopeful days of the early sixties are worthy of mention in any discussion of that era, as they continue to be studiously ignored by the people who write the books and make the films and the documentaries that explain to succeeding generations what happened without telling them why it happened, leaving each generation better-informed, more knowledgeable and more profoundly ignorant than the last, having trained them to observe the spectacular effects rather than the causes of history.

To my generation the Kennedys were never given a proper burial.

Alone among the Jesus groups, we found our calling (and much of our leadership) amongst the religiously dispossessed. Treated like roadkill by the churches, judged to be reprobate, unsalvageable, in league with the Communists, beyond the redemptive powers of Jesus Christ Himself, the publicans and sinners of our day were easy targets for the scribes and Pharisees of our day, who loudly embraced the 10 Commandments while silently renouncing the teachings of Jesus Christ, especially the ones that tried to get them to do something besides go to church on Sunday. The "Judeo-Christian ethic," as they liked to call it, was far more Judeo than Christian. Not much had changed, religiously, in 2,000 years. The drunks and harlots were still drunks and harlots and the white sepulchres by any other name were still whited sepulchres (Matthew 23: 27).

Because we agreed with many of the aims and complaints of the counterculture, we were welcome or at least tolerated in their midst. We ourselves had nothing to lose and everything to gain by returning to this *milieu* from which we had been rescued and redeemed by the Revolutionary of all Revolutionaries, finding the dope dens and hard-rock hells that we had come out of to be fertile ground for the gospel that we alone were preaching.

"Wherefore come out from among them, and be ye separate, saith the Lord, and touch not the unclean thing; and I will receive you" (2 Corinthians 6:17).

With regard to our communal lifestyle, it was again not surprising that the C-word ("C" as in "Communist") should be hurled in our direction as well, despite the fact that we were born-again, Spirit-filled Christians whose doctrines about salvation and the Messiahship of Jesus Christ were in perfect accord with mainline Protestant fundamentalism, and notwithstanding the fact that we devoured our Bibles as we had once devoured the effluvium of the '60s. More to the point, we not only read our Bibles, a practice unheard of and incomprehensible to our parents, who faithfully regurgitated what was fed to them from the pulpits, we could quote it chapter and verse as we had once quoted the lyrics of Dylan and the Beatles.

Worst of all we were doing it in public, where angels and timid Christians feared to tread, proving that the Word of God was not only "mighty to the pulling down of strongholds" (2 Corinthians 10: 4), but that it was "of the people, for the people, and by the people" if you were fool enough to give it a public voice. You could "tell it and think it and speak it and breathe it" whether anybody but God wanted you to or not. Common men and women with uncommon goals and aspirations were proving on the streets of every major city in America that you could "earnestly contend for the faith" (Jude 1: 3) in a land that had turned its faith over to the government and the military and to the religious institutions that were lock, stock and barrel in league with the government and the military.

Perhaps typically of my generation, it wasn't until I was being trained to kill Communists that it occurred to me that I owed it to myself and to my country, perhaps even to the Communists themselves, to find out what they believed. I was curious to see how much of Marxist doctrine,

I'm the white boy in the middle of the second row. Behind me, top row, second from the right, is SSG Sherriedale Morgan, our coach. Sergeant James Wallington, top row, second from the left, has just returned from the Rome Olympics where he won a bronze medal in the welterweight division. Sergeant Ed "the talking horse" Brown, second from the right, bottom row, and the fellow standing behind me and to my left in the top row, were my two regular sparring partners.

as it was written, jived with what I had been told about it, since nothing else in my military experience jived with what I had been told about it.

I was on the boxing team at the time, stationed at Fort Bragg, North Carolina. It was the first time in seven months of non-stop training (Basic, AIT, Jump School, Phase I Special Forces) that I had time to read or the opportunity to read without being watched. I had my own room, we were off from nine in the morning after roadwork and breakfast until three in the afternoon when we had to be in the gym. Evenings were off, weekends were off.

Politics and economics were not my cup of tea but I had stopped reading fiction by this time—there was no longer anything fictional about my life once I stepped into the uniform and closed the door behind me—and Marx's long, convoluted sentences, translated from the German, proved to be good brain exercise, a worthy intellectual challenge in the midst of my physical exertions.

Exactly six years later Jesus showed up and changed everything. This miracle of miracles, this beginning of miracles, took place, curiously enough, while I was reading something about the Soviet film version of *War and Peace*. I won't go into that now except to say that the next day I went shopping for a Bible. It may have taken me two or three days to get through the Gospels. I'm a fairly fast reader and the raunchy King James fell easily on my ears, but I had to go back and re-read most of it, not sure that what I was hearing for the first time was what I was really hearing. This red-letter Jesus was nothing like the red, white and blue Jesus that I had grown up with.

The scribes and Pharisees, on the other hand, were exactly like the red, white and blue scribes and Pharisees that I had grown up with, including the ones that I had grown up with in the military, namely the chaplains, whose job, simply put, was to make sure that I and the rest of the herd were clear about whose side God was on.

This was 1968, so the likelihood—the certainty—that some of us were going to wind up dead and dismembered in the jungle naturally raised questions about the afterlife, and this too fell to the chaplaincy. As ordained priests and ministers as well as staff-level officers, most of them captains— we had to salute them as well as listen to them—they were uniquely equipped to deal with these and other extra-military concerns: prostitution, venereal disease, masturbation, drunkenness, drugs, etc., and to assure us that a hero's welcome—Nay, a martyr's welcome!—was waiting for us on the other side, beyond the body bag.

This could have triggered some tricky theological questions were it not for the fact that we were no longer civilians. We were still Catholics and Protestants, Jews and Muslims etc.—it said so on our dogtags—but our asses belonged to Uncle Sam now. My ass and the chaplain's ass. Logically it followed that our immortal souls belonged to him too. All you had to do was believe it. If you did not believe it, and if you did believe, as I did, that the chaplains were bought and paid for by the government, then you were "in deep shit."

Most of the time it would be up around our knees, sometimes clear up to our chins or even higher, but even when we were completely submerged in it, such as when the Special Forces chaplain was addressing us—an ordained priest as well as a full-fledged Green Beret— something would kick in inside of you, a kind of involuntary nervous reaction. I didn't know what to call it at the time. The military word for it was "insubordination," which was fine with me. It had a nice ring to it. I can think of a verse now that describes it even better (Job 32: 8), but I didn't know any verses back then. I had read my share of Hemingway though. For him it was a kind of literary device—"a built-in shit-detector," he called it—and I liked the sound of that even better.

Whatever it was and whatever you decided to call it, it left me with little sympathy for the chaplains, for the admittedly difficult task they faced in selling an unpopular war to a generation of misfits: the nasty task of greasing the tracks of the war machine.

The kicker for me personally was the eight years that I had spent in Catholic school. The Sisters of Notre Dame and the Christian Brothers of Ireland had left me with a better than rudimentary understanding of Catholic doctrine. Perhaps better than anybody in "A" Company, Special Forces Training Group—the only trainee who went to mass every Sunday—I knew that what the Catholic chaplain was offering us in the name of God-and-Country was a military-grade Plenary Indulgence.

Those of you who have not been Catholics will be as unfamiliar with this doctrine as my classmates in Special Forces were. It was and is a peculiarity of the Catholic religion. It's all about Heaven and Hell and how to get there. ("Plenary" is taken from the Latin *plenus*, meaning "full" or "complete." To "indulge," of course, means "to yield to" or "to satisfy the desire of"; in this case the desire to stay out of Hell.)

In my day a Plenary Indulgence was the only surefire way to go straight to Heaven: no Purgatory, no Limbo, straight to the arms of Mother Mary. Why was this important? Because Purgatory was no joyride, that's why. It was the same as Hell, same torment, only it had an end, like the Army did. And you had to be a Catholic to get one. Why was this important? Because the chaplain was now offering it to *everybody*! Every swinging dick! All you had to do was get wasted by Charlie first. You could march up to St. Peter at the Pearly Gates with your battle scars and your posthumous Purple Heart, look him straight in the eye, and tell him to (stand aside)!

God had a big soft spot in His heart for American KIAs.

For the record, I never knew a Catholic who went straight to Heaven on the wings of a Plenary Indulgence, not one, and I knew a lot of good Catholics. Mrs. Hallstone, our next-door neighbor on San Antonio Drive in Salinas—they were 804, we were 808—was the only one who even came close.

Nobody from the government came to her door and handed it to her on a silver platter, either, a reward for her diehard patriotism. She had to get it the way you got everything in the Catholic religion, and nothing was harder to get or a bigger prize when you got it than a Plenary Indulgence.

It took her weeks of hardcore dedication: 6:30 masses (weekday morning masses, not Sunday masses), daily communion, weekly confession, Tuesday novenas, rosaries and more rosaries, examining her conscience at every turn, making sure she had not strayed from the State of Grace, no alcohol. I don't know if she was allowed to have "intimate relations" with Mr. Hallstone during this time but there was no touching yourself in an impure manner or thinking any impure thoughts whether you were married or not. And no cussing!

Every Catholic schoolboy dreamed of getting one because it was the only way to avoid either Purgatory or Hell. Mine would have to be conferred miraculously, supernaturally, in my sleep. I would wake up one morning and there it would be!—hanging around my neck, tangled in my scapular, signed by Pope Pius the Twelfth. I would make it to confession one last time on Saturday, then to communion on Sunday, where I would either drop dead at the communion rail, the host dissolving on my tongue—my poor mother!—or maybe get run over by a truck crossing the street after mass. Sudden death, sudden glory! Because the longer you waited, the closer you came to your next mortal sin. Then you had to start all over again, like the guy pushing the boulder up the mountain.

Not even my mother tried to get one, as serious a Catholic as she was. "Serious" as opposed to merely "devout" like my father was. My mother stayed awake during mass. It turned out she didn't need one after all because she ended up praying with me to receive Jesus during one of my father's tirades, PTL. ("Surely the wrath of man shall praise thee. The remainder of wrath shalt Thou restrain."—Psalm 76: 10)

And I hate to say this about Mrs. Hallstone, but hers didn't do her a damned bit of good! Why? Because she didn't die quick enough, that's why. Because a Plenary Indulgence was only good until your next mortal sin, as I already pointed out. One slipup and you were "back in the shitcan," as my brother Richard used to say. And Mrs. Hallstone lived a long time after that. She might still be alive for all I know. And my father wasn't the only one in the neighborhood with a temper!—as her son Kenny can tell you.

While I do credit my Catholic upbringing with making me impervious to the military/industrial/religious horseshit they were feeding us in the name of God and Country, I don't say you had to be a Catholic to figure this out. A good buddy of mine, PFC Stuart Golden, from Nashua, New Hampshire, the Honor Graduate from Phase I and Phase II Training (Special Forces Medics, Class of '69), a born doctor if I ever saw one, figured it out before I did and he was an atheist. A philosophy major in college, he expected the Army to be lying to him. I didn't. He expected the chaplains to be hirelings. I didn't. He expected as much from the Special Forces chaplain, for example, the guy that I was serving mass for every week, as he would have from the foul-mouthed buck sergeant who ran the "A" Company mess hall, whose daily culinary offerings were on a par with the rest of our diet.

Maybe you did have to be a Catholic to get pissed off about it—I don't know. I do know the nuns would have been pissed. Father Earley (Monsignor Thomas J., pastor at Sacred Heart Parish in Salinas while I was growing up), would have taken the Special Forces chaplain out behind the mess hall and given him what Jesus gave to the moneychangers.

Sadly for me, the only Jesus I knew by this time was the Catholic-American Jesus, the flag-waving, Communist-hating Son of God. Sadder still was the fact that I never questioned it. I questioned everything else but never this. I gave other people the benefit of the doubt, but not Jesus. He was who they said He was. But unlike my friend Stu, whose disgust with religion was absolute, I couldn't pretend that Jesus didn't exist. The nuns had done too good a job on us. The stories they told us about the Man who went about everywhere doing good—healing the sick, raising the dead, turning the water into wine at His Mother's behest, catching fish when nobody else could, whipping the moneychangers like Lash LaRue, letting the children sit on His lap—were too good *not* to be true.

But Catholic schoolchildren grow up and the Catholic Jesus never does. He never becomes a man among men, never says or does anything that His mother wouldn't approve of. I was about to do plenty that *my* mother wouldn't approve of!—and where was the valiant Son of Man now when I needed Him?

So there was this "dichotomy," as Stu would have put it. I was barking up the wrong tree, as usual. The ass-kicking Messiah that I was looking for didn't exist, and the one who did exist wasn't going to re-write history to suit me. It turned out He was listening though. Once I was ready to stop barking and finally start listening myself, that was all it took for Him to get His foot in the door. (Revelation 3:20) It was worth the wait.

In the meantime I had no Catholic aces up my sleeve. I was prepared, however, to remind St. Peter, the first Pope, of my near-perfect attendance record. He could send me to Hell for any number of unconfessed mortal sins, but one thing he couldn't get me for was missing mass on Sunday! Not once in 16 years! Not deliberately!

Which was more than *he* could say.

Immediately following the Gospels, in my new life as a born-again, thrilled-to-be-alive Christian, I came to the Book of Acts, Luke's account of the adventures of the Early Church. I was a new creature in Christ Jesus now —"Old things are passed away; behold, all things are become new!" (2 Corinthians 5: 17)—but the idea that I had been lied to so pervasively for so many years was hard to shake.

Now I was in for another healthy surprise, this time a political surprise. I was about to find out that Karl Marx, the author of everything that Capitalist America loves to hate, had gotten his infernal ideas—"From each according to his ability; to each according to his need."—straight out of the New Testament!

"And all that believed were together, and had all things common, and sold their possessions and goods, and parted them to all men, as every man had need." (Acts 2: 44, 45)

"And the multitude of them that believed were of one heart and one soul: neither said any of them that ought of the things which he possessed was his own; but they had all things common." (Acts 4: 32)

"Neither was there any among them that lacked: for as many as were possessors of lands or houses sold them, and brought the prices of the things that were sold, and laid them down at the apostles' feet: and distribution was made according as every man had need." (Acts 4: 34)

Why had nobody told us this? Why had none of our teachers, none of our pastors, none of our professors, none of our political leaders—and of course none of our parents—breathed a word to us about this obvious, literal connection between commune-ism and primitive Christian socialism? Was it because they hadn't read it? That must have been it.

Some of them had read the Bible—my father claimed to have read it—and some of them had read Marx, but not many of them had read both Marx and the Bible, and the ones who had weren't talking about it.

My professors in the English Department at Fresno State were the only ones I knew who had read both Marx and the Bible. I heard them speak intelligently about both schools of thought, both *genres*, but never in the same sentence. Was this because they couldn't put two and two together? I found this hard to believe. If anybody could take apart the English language and put it back together again, it was these guys. They could take apart a whole book, a complicated work of fiction, like an auto mechanic taking apart an engine, cleaning and repairing or replacing each component as necessary, and putting it all back together again in perfect working order in the front of the customer—the student—in 55 minutes or less.

The authors of these faulty manuscripts, on the other hand, the men and women who designed and built the engines that powered the vehicle of their thoughts, didn't have a clue what was going on inside their own contraptions!

Hemingway, for example. The poor devil thought he liked to hunt and fish! He thought he liked women! He thought he liked canned peaches! Little did he know that his guns and his fishing poles and his thirst for manly adventure were mere phallic expressions of a deep-seated, un-fuck-ing-thinkable desire for other men!

He wasn't trout fishing with his buddy Bill in Spain. He wasn't shooting ducks in Italy or humping it in the boonies with his wife in Africa. He was getting even with his mother for making him play the cello!

I found it hard to believe that these Doctors of Letters, these literary surgeons, could possibly have missed the obvious, literal connection between Marx's principle thesis—the equal distribution of wealth—and the primary social construct of the Early Church; along with, of course, the even more dangerous implication that commune-ism and socialism, per se, are no more inherently evil than capitalism or democracy, per se, are inherently righteous.

We ended up doing it anyway whether anybody wanted us to or not. Some of us are still doing it. It may not be the easiest way to live (although it might be); or the most comfortable way to live (although it might be); and it's certainly not the most popular way to live, democratically speaking; but it is, without a doubt, the cheapest, most cost-effective way of going into all the world and preaching the Gospel to every creature (Mark 16: 15), which is probably why it worked so well in the beginning.

We are not the same body of believers that we were 20 or 30 years ago, or even five or 10 years ago. Our bodies have changed (mine just turned 70), our witnessing tactics have changed. But the fire that burned in our young bosoms wasn't put there by us and it won't die because of us or because of our children, who have their own histories and their own stories to tell.

Mine begins shortly. Two women have read parts of it; one a believer, the other a semi-believer. The believer is a long-time friend and associate, a nice Jewish girl turned Jesus freak. The semi-believer is a retired editor for Wiley Publications (*Books for Dummies*), wife of an Army buddy. The believer suggested that I keep the two parts of my testimony separate: before and since the Family. The book editor suggested that a simple explanation of my involvement with the Family would be helpful to the reader.

I have decided to take the book editor's advice on this, which is what you're reading here if you're still reading. While I do appreciate the wisdom in not aligning oneself too closely with an outfit that continues to be number one on a good many Christian shit-lists, I am constitutionally incapable of being more than one person at a time.

If we are the sum of our experiences, the best part of me belongs to the Family.

★"Surely the wrath of man shall praise Thee: the remainder of wrath shalt Thou restrain."

CHAPTER ONE:

STEINBECK COUNTRY

My father was a banker, the son of Italian immigrants, born in America but raised and educated in Italy. My mother was also of Italian descent. Good Catholics, they sent my brothers to parochial school in Monterey, California, which at that time was still a fishing village—famous for its sardine runs—the setting for Steinbeck's *Tortilla Flat* and *Cannery Row*. Richard was born in 1936, Gary in 1941, and I came along just before the end of war in 1945, the last of three sons.

When I was three years old we moved 17 miles inland to Salinas, where Steinbeck's *East of Eden* was conceived and later filmed and where I too attended parochial schools. Gary set batting records his senior year at Palma High that hadn't been broken as of a few years ago: highest batting average (.420), most doubles and triples, most homeruns, most RBIs. Richard joined the Navy when he was 18 and I graduated at the top of my seventh-grade class.

When I was 13 we left "Steinbeck country" for the hot, dry interior of California known as the San Joaquin Valley. My father was moving up in the banking community and I was about to get my first taste of the American public school system. The nearest Catholic high school was 40 miles away, a boarding school in Fresno, and neither my parents nor I wanted me to leave home, so the matter was settled as far as I was concerned. I had no particular qualms about attending public school until my father, the night before I was to begin my freshman year at Hanford High, took me aside after dinner and began to describe for me, in his effusive manner, the benefits of a secular education.

"Life in the real world is about to begin for you! Not only that, it's going to be the best thing that ever happened to you!"

My teenage alarm bells went off for the first time, and I began to wonder, for the first time, not so much about the world that I was about to enter, but about the one I was leaving. If public school—which I had always equated with Protestantism—was the real world, then what was the world that I had been living in for the past 14 years?

What about the Catechism that I had memorized? What about the Latin that I had memorized to become an altar boy?—sitting on the couch every evening with my father while he drilled me in the correct pronunciation of the Latin because no son of his was going to murder the language the way those Irish priests did! All that slaving away to make straight A's to please my father—did all that amount to nothing?

I soon found out what was real and what wasn't. Fighting, sports, sex, cussing, money, all the things that make a man a monkey in the System, all that was real enough. My Catholic upbringing? Forget it. By the time I finished high school and was ready for college, I was already well on my way to becoming the foul-mouthed, crass American that I've had to fight against ever since.

With my grades I could have gone to a larger, more prestigious institute of higher learning (sic) than the one I went to, a medium-sized state college that specialized in agriculture, but I had no ambitions education-wise other than to please my parents. As early as high school I was pretty well convinced that the useful part of my education had ended in the seventh grade. I still can't think of anything I learned after that—except for learning how to type my senior year in high school—that's been of any earthly use to me. My BA in journalism probably kept me from getting killed in Vietnam, but apart from that I can't think of anything I learned in seven years of college that I wouldn't trade for a two-week faith trip in the Family.

I majored in Business to please my father, hated it, and changed to Journalism because I liked to write. In my freshman year I joined a fraternity and spent the next three years on Greek Row. Except for myself, one Korean kid, one from Israel and one from Whittier—Nixon's hometown—everybody in this fraternity was either a farmer, a cattle rancher, a dairyman, or a grape-grower; sons and grandsons of the European and Asian immigrants who had come west around the turn of the century and within 50 years had turned California's sagebrush and jackrabbit land into the richest, most diverse farming region in the world.

I don't know how many of them are still farmers—I doubt very many—but at the time they were very gung-ho about it, hitting the books hard all week and heading home on weekends to help out on the farm, unless there was a rodeo. And once a year there was an important fraternity function that we all had to attend—the Pink Rose Formal—but rodeos and fraternity functions were few and far between for the brethren of Alpha Gamma Rho.

On weekends while my farmer friends were home pulling tractor duty, fixing fences, hauling hay, milking, irrigating, pruning, "eating their bread"—and staying in school—"by the sweat of the brow" (Genesis 3: 19), I, the banker's son, would be out either hunting or fishing, depending on the season, or working on my suntan or my physique.

Compared to me and probably compared to most college-age Americans, my farmer friends had some serious interests in life. They were serious about school, for one thing, because it was part of what they'd be doing for the rest of their lives: preparation for the growingly sophisticated, ruthlessly competitive world of modern agriculture.

They were serious about girls and dating like they were about everything else, taking a keen, rather straightforward interest in the opposite sex. They'd been judging livestock all their lives and knew a good straight-backed heifer when they saw one!

Now they're the alumni, the old farts who come to the meetings on Monday night and reminisce about the good old days. "Good old AGR! Best years of our lives!"—serious about all the things that didn't make a damned bit of sense to me, and still don't.

I didn't need an education because I already had one. I already knew how to read and write and do arithmetic. Thanks to the nuns I even knew how to spell and punctuate, which put almost in the genius category next to some of my public-school-educated classmates in the Journalism Department, some of whom could barely write a coherent sentence. Graduate school (in the English Department) was even worse.

For what it was worth, I got the kind of education in parochial schools that they preach against now in the public schools in America. The way the nuns handled us, and later the Christian Brothers, with firmness and discipline, with clear behavioral guidelines and a strict academic standard—along with the wholehearted consent of our parents—would be considered child abuse in America today. You can't teach a kid anything without depriving him of some of his "rights" is what it amounts to.

My professors thought I had some ability as a writer, which was the one bright spot on my bleak, upper-middle-class horizons, but the idea of getting a job on some small-town newspaper, where the average journalism graduate is sent to learn the ropes—where they teach you how to think like a 12-year-old in order to communicate effectively with mainstream America—was absolute death to me.

When it came time to graduate I had two options. One, I could go to graduate school and continue my deferment from the Army—this was 1967, with the Vietnam War in full swing—or I could volunteer for the draft and get it over with. I was sick of school, so I went down and volunteered for the draft.

To backtrack a little, a few months before I graduated I began to look for another branch of the service to get into besides the Army. One of my fraternity brothers had signed up for the Navy Reserves, a two-year hitch that sounded like a better deal than what the Army was offering, so I went down and tried that first.

I took the written test one evening and was interviewed afterward by a fellow from the Navy who told me, politely but firmly, that they couldn't take me because of my speech impediment. I stuttered. I had stuttered all my life and this wasn't the first time somebody had noticed it, but it was the first time that anybody in authority had told me to my face that I wouldn't be able to cut the mustard in a man's world. Determined to prove that I *could* cut it, I arranged to meet with the Marine Corps recruiter on campus one day, to see about Marine Corps OCS, but he told me the same thing.

There were two ways I could have looked at it. I could have looked at it any sane hippy would have looked at it, or the way my mother would have looked at it—as a gift straight from the hand of God—because if the Navy and the Marines didn't want me, there was a good chance the Army wouldn't take me either, which meant I could have gotten me out of the service altogether, out of the draft, but these kinds of thoughts never entered my head. If they did I quickly got them *out* of my head. I had never seen my speech impediment as anything but a curse—straight from the hand of God—and wasn't about to start looking on the bright side now that my country needed me.

As it turned out, I could have gone down there to the recruiting office and not said a word, and the guy sitting behind the desk—the buck sergeant with the crewcut and the PR album—wouldn't have noticed, he was so busy talking and showing me pictures of the Modern Army. He didn't get many college-educated suckers like me.

He showed me color photos of the kind of barracks I'd be living in. They looked just like the dormitory I had stayed in my freshman year at Fresno State. Good old Homan Hall! Same kind of bricks. By the time he finished blowing smoke up my legs I had signed up for three years instead of two.

This was late 1967. I was 22 years old, a college-educated sucker, a soon-to-be soldier and an erstwhile member of the '60s generation. I looked up the word "erstwhile" because I've never used it before. It says "former" or "formerly," which isn't what I was trying to say. I wasn't *formerly* a member of the '60s generation because I *never* belonged to it, and neither did anybody else I knew. We were situated right in the middle of it—Fresno is about halfway between L.A. and San Francisco, the two hotbeds of sedition for the western United States back in the '60s (that's about 250 miles in either direction, about as far as Slovenia is from Germany)—and that's as close as I ever got to the '60s.

I watched it on the Six O'Clock News, with Chet Huntley and David Brinkley, and read about it in the *San Francisco Chronicle*, but it could have been happening on another planet as far as I was concerned.

You've seen the movie *Field of Dreams*. Remember the scene at the PTA meeting? Kevin Costner's wife is getting into it with this lady. The other lady is upset about a book that she wants to see removed from the school library. She's never read the book, written during the '60s by a black fellow who later figures prominently in the film, but Mrs. Costner has read it. and calls the other lady a "Nazi cow" under her breath.

Then she comes to the point. The trouble with the other lady, she says, is that she had never "experienced the sixties."

Oh yes she had!

"No," Mrs. Costner says with finality. "You never experienced the sixties. You had two fifties and went right on into the seventies."

That was me. I had two fifties and went right on into the Army. Two weeks after I graduated from Fresno State, I was taking basic training at Fort Lewis, Washington.

CHAPTER TWO:

BAD NEWS IN BABYLON

I didn't hate the Army immediately. It hated me immediately but it took me a while to get the point, three days to be exact. The swearing-in ceremony at the Induction Center in Fresno was Thursday, February 15th. Three days later—Sunday, February 18th—was my first day off in the Army. I was standing behind the barracks watching the sun go down—watching my life go down the drain—when I had what I would call my first spiritual experience.

Those of you who have not watched the sun go down on a military compound haven't missed much. For me it was a way of reminding myself that I was still human, still capable of enjoying the good things in life. It had rained every day for the past week—it rained every day the entire two months that I was stationed at Fort Lewis—but it wasn't raining now, and I was determined not to let my dreary surroundings get the better of me. I had just gotten off the phone to my parents. I had the feeling they were proud of me; at least my father was. My mother had better sense along these lines.

Fort Lewis was a big place, occupying I don't know how many hundreds of thousands of acres in the Pacific Northwest. Like all military installations it was laid out like a city, with its own residential areas, called barracks; its own restaurants, called mess halls; its own recreational facilities, called firing ranges; its own system of transportation, its own postal system, its own judicial system, its own medical system, etc. etc. Its own System, period.

There's not much you can't get on an Army base: booze, drugs, sex, an education, you name it. The only thing you can't get is freedom, but freedom is not something that comes knocking on your door in civilian life, either, which I believe is what the Lord was trying to show me that day; because all of a sudden, in my mind's eye, I wasn't looking at an Army base anymore, a military compound, but at a very small, scaled-down version of the entire country, of America itself.

In biblical terms, in the language I'm familiar with now, I saw Babylon the Whore reduced to her essence. The America I was looking at was a war machine, a military/industrial complex, which is what the hippies had been saying all along. That was the substance of my revelation: the hippies were right. And if the hippies were right, that meant that everything that I had ever believed or wanted to believe was wrong. It was a simple equation, one that a complicated fool like me could understand. I had been marching all my life, taking orders all my life, thinking everybody's thoughts but my own, or worse, thinking that I had been capable of thinking for myself.

I had been brainwashed pure and simple—by experts.

CHAPTER THREE:

THREE YEARS TO KILL

I now had three years to kill if they didn't kill me first. The weekly body count for Americans in January/February, 1968 was about 500, with maybe five times that many wounded; not a happy statistic if you had just seen the end of everything you had once been willing to kill for and die for.

One of the first things I did in Basic was sign up for OCS. With my degree I could become a second lieutenant in six months and still get out in three years. I figured if I had to do something I hated, I might as well get paid for it. Second lieutenants were making maybe four times what I was getting as a Private E-1. Plus—and this was a big plus—I wouldn't be living with the same bunch of animals that I was living with now, 60% of whom were in the Army as an alternative to spending two years in prison.

Something else the recruiter forgot to mention was that I was being assigned to an "experimental company." The experiment would be to see how two college boys, myself and another fellow (Bill Hewitt, his name was. He had a Master's degree in Business from the University of Santa Clara.), would get along with the riff-raff of American society.

These riff-raff, of course, were the unhappy sons of the Republic that the system couldn't do anything with except to make criminals out of them, first all, and then foot-soldiers, infantrymen, useful to their country for one thing.

When I got to Vietnam myself I met a Red Cross worker who had something to do with inspecting the morgue on the Da Nang Air Base. She told me rather matter-of-factly that 10% of the officers being killed in the war—first and second lieutenants mostly, white college boys like myself—were being shot in the back or hand-grenaded by the people who were supposed to be following them into battle.

I believed this to be a conservative, hopeful estimate, my own life having been threatened on more than one occasion while I was still a Private E-1.

CHAPTER FOUR:

CUTTING THE MUSTARD

In addition to being part of an experimental company, I was chosen, along with four other trainees, to lead my platoon. I had taken a year and a half of ROTC (Air Force Reserve Officer's Training Corps) at Fresno State, so I already knew how to march and call cadence, making me the logical candidate for platoon guide. As platoon guide I was made an "acting E-6," or staff sergeant, with a black-and-yellow elastic band around my arm denoting my rank. My pay grade didn't change but I had the responsibility of running the lives of my platoon-mates when Sergeant First Class Dean or one of the other duty sergeants weren't around, which was occasionally throughout the day and every night after chow until reveille the following morning.

Below me were four acting-E-5's, or buck sergeants, who became my squad leaders. I gave the commands when we were marching or running from place to place and the secondary commands when the real NCOs were present. I also caught most of the guff that would otherwise have been directed at the lifers.

One of my squad leaders was a mild-mannered, studious fellow named Robles. He was waiting to use the phone one evening outside the mess hall when he was accosted by one of the worst troublemakers in the platoon, a fellow named Ohotto, Donald Ohotto.

Later that evening inside the barracks, Ohotto and Smith, another accomplished troublemaker, threatened to beat the shit out of Robles and no ass-kissing sonofabitch, meaning me, was going to stop them.

With nobody to tell me what to do, SFC Dean having gone home for the evening, leaving me in charge at the zoo, I offered Smith and Ohotto the chance to kick *my* ass if they thought they could, if they wanted to go through me to get to Robles. By this time everybody had moved to the top of the stairwell, next to the room that Robles and I and the other squad leaders slept in. I had told him to go inside and not to come out. I then took my armband off and told both of them in front of the entire platoon that nobody would get in trouble for doing to me what they were threatening to do to Robles, halfway hoping they would take me up on it.

With everybody watching, hoping to see a little honest bloodletting for a change, it must have occurred to both of them that I wasn't the only one who thought they needed a good beating, and they both backed down, as I thought they would. Although I had never physically demonstrated that I could kick anybody's ass, I must have acted like I could, which was all it usually took in the Army; probably one of the reasons the VC and the NVA were doing such a nifty job of kicking our asses in Vietnam. They acted like they weren't afraid of us.

Later on I did get the chance to demonstrate my ass-kicking ability when one of the platoon guides from a neighboring company, hearing about the altercation in our barracks, challenged me to some lighthearted fisticuffs one rainless Sunday afternoon.

Word was going around, no doubt spread by my opponent, that I would be getting into the ring with a former Golden Gloves champion. He was from one of the Midwestern states, maybe Iowa or Ohio, one of those. I had no way of knowing if any of this was true or not, of course. You hear a lot of stories in the Army and this was one of them. I did know that this fellow belonged to the best company in the battalion—best marchers, least troublesome, most obedient—and he had the best platoon, possibly due to his leadership. I can't remember which platoon we were. We were the jailbird platoon.

I had done a little boxing myself in college. Fresno State didn't have a boxing team but my uncle Fred (Bianchi, my mother's brother) was a well-known professional trainer. Whenever I had time off from school I would visit my brother Richard in the city—he lived in the Marina district—and Fred would let me use the gym, Newman's Gym on Leavenworth Street.

Fred was regarded by his colleagues—Enoch Yip, for example—as one of the best teachers in the business. He had worked with a number of good fighters, including Bobo Olson when he was middleweight champion. He was in Olson's corner in the three fights with Robinson, and in Eddie Machen's corner in Stockholm the night Ingemar Johansson knocked him out in the first round, leading to the title fight with Patterson.

Fred was everybody's favorite uncle. My father didn't like him. Women liked him. Blonde and blue-eyed, he looked more Swedish than Italian. His sister—my mother—said he looked just like Paul Newman, the movie actor.

We would see him on the *Friday Night Fights* working somebody's corner in Madison Square Garden or Vegas or London. My mother would wrap her fingers around her thumb and make a fist!

"That's my brother!"

If nothing else I considered myself to be an avid student of the sport. I had no business getting in the ring with an accomplished amateur, if that's what this fellow was, but I had never heard of anybody from the Midwest amounting to much in the boxing world. Partly because of this and partly because he was a white boy, but mostly because I felt like hitting somebody, I was happy to take him up on his offer.

The ring was a circle formed by my platoon on one side and his on the other. We were wearing 12-ounce gloves, both of us middleweights. I had a height and reach advantage. My opponent was what you would call a "busy" fighter, the kind that comes straight in at you. I had an educated left hand—educated by my Uncle Fred—that I stuck in his face a number of times, trying to set him up for the right, but he quit with a bloody nose before the first round was over, much to everybody's disappointment, especially mine. It wasn't much of a fight. Both Smith and Ohotto were in the crowd and never gave me any trouble after that, although they continued to persecute Robles.

CHAPTER FIVE:

SILVER WINGS

Basic Training was eight weeks, followed by 10 weeks of AIT (Advanced Individual Training) at Fort Ord, California, a few miles up the beach from where I was born. Again I was made platoon guide and again I was challenged, this time by a long-armed gorilla who threatened to relieve me of my white nuts one of these dark nights, but he too backed down when I offered him the chance of do it publicly.

By this time I knew I wasn't cut out to be an officer—or a gentleman—no matter how much they paid me, so I was looking around for something less gentlemanly to do. One day the Special Forces recruiter came around and gave his spiel to each of the infantry companies and I signed up for that, waiving my OCS.

This was around the time that Bobby Kennedy was killed. Across the road from the barracks I slept in at Fort Ord was a snack bar with a juke box. Procul Harem's "Whiter Shade of Pale" could sometimes be heard above the bark and growl of military life.

"I was feelin' kinda sea-sick… The crowwwwd called out for morrre…"

From AIT I was sent to jump school at Fort Benning, Georgia, and from there to the John F. Kennedy Center for Special Warfare at Fort Bragg, North Carolina, Home of Special Forces Training Group.

They told us we were the largest incoming class in Special Forces history. There were 180 of us to begin with, something like that, maybe two or three times the usual number. One of the reasons for this, I believe, was the '68 Tet Offensive, when Communist forces, led by General Giap (the same general who had overrun the French in the battle of Dien Bien Phu), overran the Americans up and down the country, inflicting the worst casualties of the war so far, and of course stirring up the war-minded youth of America, who greatly outnumbered the hippies.

Another reason for this large influx of Special Forces recruits was the release that same year of a film called *The Green Berets*, starring John Wayne, which became a big box-office hit as well as a topnotch propaganda tool for the Army. I say this in retrospect, not having seen the movie personally, but I saw the effect it had on the ones who did, which was everybody I knew in Special Forces, including the chaplain and the sergeant major. It was definitely on the recommended list, which didn't surprise me.

What did surprise me was how little difference there was between the way the troops reacted to it—guys like me who had been in the Army about six months—and the way the cadre reacted to it.

My Collins Pocket Dictionary defines cadre as "a nucleus of trained men around which a military or political unit can be built." I think that's the way I looked at it then. I wasn't looking for role models but I did expect that "a nucleus of trained men" would have a little better sense about some things than we did. About the war, for example. You'd naturally think that, wouldn't you? You'd think if there was anybody in the freaking Army who could tell the difference between a serious war movie and B-grade Hollywood hype, it would be these guys, these lifers, these elite; considered in those days to be amongst the *crème de la crème* of America's fighting forces, along with the Rangers and the Navy SEALs. Every one of them had been to Vietnam at least once. Every one of them had the medals and the scars to prove it. Bronze Stars and Purple Hearts were a dime-a-dozen in this outfit—everybody had at least one of those— but there were also more Silver Stars and DSCs (Distinguished Service Crosses), I'd venture to say, amongst the Special Forces cadre, than you'd find anyplace else in the Army outside of Arlington Cemetery.

But apparently they couldn't tell, or, if they could, the stroke job that Hollywood was giving them was too much for them. I heard these same hardcore professionals, these "legends in their own lifetime," talking about that stupid movie like it was an Army training film, and John Wayne like he was one of their bosom buddies, a regular comrade-in-arms.

CHAPTER SIX:

WHILE WE'RE ON THE SUBJECT

While we're on the subject, I'd have to say that I've seen the same strange phenomenon at work in the Family in recent years, the same mindless enthusiasm for Hollywood that I saw amongst my cohorts in the Green Berets.

When you think about it—when you consider who we are, or who we're supposed to be— who we used to be—it's almost inconceivable that so many of us could have so little sense when it comes to Hollywood. If I didn't know better, if I hadn't spent the better part of my adult life reading Mo Letters, I'd be tempted to think that we were no better-equipped to deal with the delusions of the film world than the meatheads in Special Forces were.

That's not what I get tempted to think, though, having served in both armies. Having hated the one and loved the other, what I get tempted to think sometimes is that "those who were once enlightened, and have tasted of the heavenly gift, and were made partakers of the Holy Ghost, and have tasted the good Word of God, and the powers of the world to come" (Hebrews 6: 4, 5) are without excuse.

What I get tempted to think sometimes is that the argument-of-choice for Family members wishing to defend their ungodly viewing habits

("Moviegoing is a *subjective* experience," they tell you, "a matter of taste and personal preference. So who's to say what's good for you and what isn't?") is the same mealy-mouthed argument I had to listen to in college, the one that my professors would drag out when called upon to defend the stupid *books* we had to read.

Twentieth Century American Literature, World Literature, Russian Literature, Contemporary American Poets, the bottom line was always the same. It was art, boys and girls; not religion. And you didn't dare mix the two, because art was freedom and religion was the *suppression* of freedom.

There was some truth to this, of course, thanks to the churches, but you didn't have to be very religious to get on the wrong side of the literary establishment. You didn't have to be very smart to figure out where all this supposed "freedom" was taking us, either, or where it's taking us today in the Family.

In college I took the traditional Catholic approach to the arts, which is that God the Father, the Omniscient, Omnipresent, Omnipotent First Person of the Trinity, has the right to meddle in human affairs if He wanted to, even in the arts if He wants to, including the literary arts— especially the literary arts because I loved books—but this kind of logic got me nowhere with my professors, who let me know, politely but firmly, that they were "inhospitable to such beliefs" and that I would do well to put my brain to better use.

If I didn't start putting it to better use, they warned me, I would not only be failing to realize my full intellectual potential, which was bad enough, I would be falling prey to the cardinal intellectual blunder; admitting, in effect, that I couldn't *think for myself,* which was almost the worst thing anybody could say about you in those days, just like today.

What the art worshippers don't like to admit, and what a lot of people in the Family don't like to be reminded of, is something that Dad brought out once upon a time when he was defending his own right to teach. Thinking for yourself, he said, always involves somebody *telling* you what to think for yourself. You always wind up listening to somebody one way or the other, sooner or later. (TO THE MEDIA—FROM A GURU— ABOUT THE SECTS: "Whose Fool Are You?" —GP 800)

For whatever reason—stubbornness, my own intellectual pride, my

Catholic upbringing—I couldn't bring myself to accept what my professors in the English Department were telling me, most of them. I couldn't buy it in the Army, either, that grown men could be so easily seduced, "drawn away of their own lusts, and enticed" (James 1: 14), and I sure as Hell can't buy it here in the Family where people are supposed to have a modicum of spirituality even if they're not very worldly-wise.

I think it's a simple matter of discernment—either you have it or you don't—and from what I've seen, a lot of people don't have it, especially not on video night. Either they don't want it—because they're not willing to pay the price, not willing to suffer "persecution for righteousness' sake" (Matthew 10: 36), the persecution of peer pressure, which is almost the worst kind there is as far as I'm concerned—or maybe they're just too proud to admit they don't have it, because that would be admitting that somebody else *does* have it. It would mean submitting to somebody's better judgment, which of course is anathema to the artistic conscience.

As busy as I am these days in the Industrial Arts, I consider the movie ratings to be a labor-saving device, somebody doing something for me that I don't have to do for myself. It works for me and I recommend it. I've never thought of it as Dad or Maria or Peter trying to keep their finger on us because they don't trust us, although I'm not particularly offended at the idea. But I can see where somebody with absolute faith in his own artistic integrity might be tempted to see the ratings as an intrusion into his private life, something that comes between him and the Lord and his own self-interests.

For what it's worth, I have never watched an unrated American movie that I thought was worth watching afterwards, not one. Most of them stunk so bad I couldn't get out of the room fast enough. The one or two that I did manage to sit all the way through—because somebody told me it was rated or it came highly recommended by somebody who should have known better— left me feeling the way I used to feel in college driving home from the whorehouse on Saturday night, disgusted with myself because I couldn't get a real girl.

I shared something to this effect at a Home Council Meeting recently, and most of the young people—most of the home—thought I was nuts.

"You mean you didn't like (*Waltzing Through Sodom*) just because it wasn't *rated*? You didn't dig (*Airheads Rule!*) just because it wasn't approved by WS? C'mon, gimme a break!"

But it's true. I didn't like them not because they weren't rated, I didn't like them because I didn't *like* them. I wouldn't have liked them if they *had* been rated, but for some reason there aren't many rated videos that I don't like. There aren't many that I get to see, either, not in this home, not since the voting majority started watching two, three, four videos a week downstairs in their own rooms, plus the weekly pilgrimage to the cinema.

"Video night" rolls around—that's my appointed evening to watch something besides the backs of my eyelids—and everybody's seen everything. I might as well not even show up unless I want to watch some clunker just because it's new or because Brad Pitt is in it. That's my dilemma. What I'm allowed or not allowed to watch—unitedly, with the rest of the Home—has nothing to do with either the movie ratings or the "dictatorial policies" of WS,★ and everything to do with the "tastes and personal preferences" of the people I'm living with.

It's got something to do with their *appetites*, too.

ap•pe•tite (ap′¹ t²t′) 1. a desire to satisfy some craving of the body; specif., a desire for food,   or, sometimes, a desire for some specific food 2. any strong desire or craving [an appetite for knowledge]

taste (noun)

1. the ability to notice, appreciate, and judge what is beautiful, appropriate, or harmonious, or what is excellent in art, music, decoration, clothing, etc.

2. ability to judge aesthetically

3. faculty of making discerning judgments in aesthetic matters

4. sense of what is proper or acceptable socially.

"The remark was in poor taste."

★WS, or World Services, was the Family's ruling body, thought by some to be "overly dictatorial." David Berg, founder and leader of the Family until his death in 1994, was the son of Virginia Brandt Berg, a contemporary of Amy Semple McPherson.

Berg's own study of scripture led him to conclude that democratic rule, rule by popular consensus, was the weakest form of government; first of all because it is unscriptural.

"Wide is the gate, and broad is the way, that leadeth to destruction," Jesus said, "and *many* there be which go in thereat; because straight is the gate, and narrow is the way, which leadeth unto life, and *few* there be that find it." (Matthew 7: 13, 14)

If these words of Jesus are true—if the majority is always wrong—it makes democratic rule (the many versus the few) a fundamentally flawed ideology; that is if Jesus was always right.

The best form of earthly government, Berg taught, was a dictatorship of the Holy Spirit   like the one that ruled in Israel under the prophet Samuel. When the children of Israel obeyed the voice of God through Samuel, they prospered and were blessed. They were doing what God wanted them to do whether they wanted to or not, which most of them didn't.

The will of the majority had always mattered more to them than the singular will of the Almighty. They wanted to be respected and feared like other nations, a power unto themselves, not to be subject to the whims of an unseen, unpredictable God; not to be the salt of the earth or the light to the Gentiles that God was trying to get them to be.

CHAPTER SEVEN:

CATS AND DOGS

Cats have taste, dogs have appetite. Watch a cat eat sometime. If it's the least bit off, 30 seconds past the expiry date, he'll turn his nose up at it and walk off in a huff. If you want to know if a piece of meat is fresh enough for you to eat or not, give some to your cat first. If he'll eat it, you can eat it—unless it's gopher meat.

A dog, on the other hand, will eat anything, including his own vomit, including a few other things that I won't mention here. You can do whatever you want to to protect a dog from his own nature—this is what a lot of people think the movie ratings are for—because you're ignorant of the fact or choose to ignore the fact that dogs, all dogs everywhere including *your* dog, are scroungers and scavengers, carrion-eaters, and have been since Noah got off the ark.

This demonstrable, provable fact, unquestioned for millennia by dog or man, is viewed with contempt by modern-day pet owners and by their patrons in the pet-food industry. The venerable, time-honored tradition of serving the family pooch scraps from the table—first the cat, then the dog, then the chickens—has been replaced by the supermarket, whole sections of which are now devoted to the canine palate, and to the idiots who think they're doing the dog a favor by treating him like he's human. An Old Testament proverb comes to mind here but I won't repeat it.

"Responsible pet owners," they like to be called, reject the notion that their canine *protégés* are exactly what they seem to be—culinary scumbags—refusing to let the poor bugger eat anything that hasn't been sanctified by the Veterinarians' Association and the International Dog Food Consortium, including a number of otherwise-intelligent Family people I know who have a higher dietary standard for their dog than they do for their kids!

The dog, of course, agrees with them. He's loyal!

"Yeah, right! No chicken bones for me! Gimme that white meat!"

He doesn't think he's a dog anymore!

But he's still a chowhound at heart and he'll demonstrate it at the first opportunity, the minute he gets off the leash and gets a whiff of that nice, rotten, maggot-infested roadkill down there decomposing in the ditch...

All that to say that I watch very few movies in the home I'm in now. The previewing committee is three people: one YA, one FGA, both team-workers, and one SGA, a former VS.★ Between the three of them they've seen every movie that's been made in the past 30 years: the Good, the Bad, and the Ugly. That's our standard. They've seen'm so it's OK for everybody else to see'm, including the 13- and 14-year-olds. The home is in a mess, about one video away from being put on probation by the CROs, and I'm ready to walk out the door while I still have the right to.

I've got nothing against Brad Pitt, by the way. When I head for the fresh air on video night, it's not because of the actors. It's because I don't go to the whorehouse anymore, not even in my own house, especially not in my own house. If other people want to do it, other members of the household, I can't stop them, but I can't help wishing they'd do it someplace else.

As for Brad Pitt, what can I say? I like the way he handles a fly rod. If I didn't know better, if I hadn't spent the better part of my pre-Family existence waving my own magic wand over the magic waters, I'd be tempted to think those were real fish he was catching in *A River Runs Through It*.

But I've seen too many hatchery fish in my day. They were putting them in California rivers as early as 50 years ago. That big one it shows him catching in the climactic fishing scene —the one that rises to a dry fly the size of a hummingbird—looked like brood stock from one of the local hatcheries, trucked in and kept alive long enough to be stuck on the end of the actor's line, is a shameful way to treat a fish if you ask me, especially one that had spent its entire existence inside a concrete pen getting milked for all he was worth. This was one time when I would have voted for catch-and-release.**

Let the poor bugger live out his days as God intended! After six months in a Montana river, if he survives that long, he'll be just as handsome and just as good to eat as his wild cousins. He'll think he's in fish heaven and he'll be right! Even a Hollywood actor, taken out of the city and transported to a Godly, clean environment, will revert to his natural state if you leave him there long enough, which of course is not the message that this movie was intended to convey.

I felt sorry for the fish. Even by Hollywood standards these were some of the sorriest-looking "trout" I think I've ever seen, half-dead, colorless rainbows that looked like they'd been raised in a penitentiary, an insult to the species and an insult to anybody who's ever thrown a fly in Montana. A little authenticity would have gone a long way in that film.

He made three good ones though, I'll say that for him: the one with Harrison Ford about the Irish, *Seven Years in Tibet*, and *Meet Joe Black*; followed, predictably, by a whole string of crummy ones. But that's just me talking. Somebody with a different set of tastes and personal preferences, or somebody with no taste at all, might look at it completely differently, which is usually what happens on video night.

By the way, in our home we don't just march off to the whorehouse on a whim. We *discuss* it first. That is to say somebody who knows a Hell of a lot more about it than I do discusses it. What I do, besides make the popcorn and get the beer, is ask the questions, which of course is an integral part of the democratic prostitutional process; leading, inexorably, to the Big Moment, the Climax (the vote).

*YA (Young Adult); FGA (First-Generation Adult); SGA (Second-Generation Adult); VS (Visiting Servant); CRO (Central Reporting Office).

**Catch-and-release is the modern-day perversion that treats God's creation as a plaything, a way for man to demonstrate his superiority over nature, his superior intellect ("I'm smarter than a fish!"), his magnanimity of spirit, his tackle, his wardrobe, and of course his camera equipment. Only the fish is playing for keeps.

CHAPTER EIGHT:

BRAD GETS THE NOD

———————————————————

This evening we have three contestants to choose from, ladies and gentlemen: one that nobody has seen, one that some of us have seen, and one that everybody has seen at least once.

The first one is held aloft, inscrutable in her gray jacket. I lead off with a provocative first question.

"What's it about?"

Looks of incredulity.

"You haven't *seen* this yet? This has been out at least six months!"

"What about this other one? It's got a good writeup in *The Grapevine*."★

"Yeah, right. My mom liked it."

I know his mom! I figure if she likes it, I probably will too. So I return to my original question.

This time he's stumped.

"It's um, like, you know… It's like… It's like howdoyousay. It's like *real slow-moving*."

Translation: It's got dialogue and a plot. You have to listen to what the actors are *saying*, as opposed to what they're doing with their guns or their fists or their…like, you know.

Brad gets the nod and I'm off to my room with my popcorn and what's left of my Karlovacko (*Kar-lo-VAHTCH-ko*, excellent Croatian lager. For a rich, high-voltage dark beer, look for the Tomislav).

Angela (that's my wife) will generally follow me out after a discreet interval. We live in the trailer out under the apple tree next to the road. After kicking the cat out ("Not on the *bed*!"), she'll let me know that she's a little miffed at my unsportsmanlike conduct at the recent United Home Activity.

"You just walk out right after the home has just voted to watch something together! Can't you just wait *five minutes*?"

Angela doesn't like cats. She doesn't like popcorn, either, or beer. Plus she's on the Teamwork. And last but not least she's German, with a strong sense of social decorum and civic responsibility, virtues that Bob and I (Bob's the cat) regrettably lack. I figure it's my time they're wasting as well as theirs.

As ill-disposed as I am toward any kind of spiritual activity on my night off (Angela will vouch for me on this), I'd sooner spend it *praying* for some of these actors than watching their silly God-damned movies! If they

Shelley, Angela, Philip, and Bob the cat, in front of our trailer in Pernice, Slovenia, 1996.

Bob guarding the bird feeder in the apple tree behind the trailer.

Me with two brown trout I caught in the creek across the road from our place in Eggersdorf, Austria, 1994.

Destroyed water wheel on the Una River, near the town of Kulen Vakuf, Bosnia, 1996. This river was named by a Roman general who, laying eyes on its exquisite, trout-filled waters, called it 'The One, the Only River.' Before the war it was a popular destination for Italian hunters and fishermen; renowned for its stag, pig, wolf and trout population. During the war it was home to a number of mass graves, courtesy of the Serb military and the Clinton administration, which sat on its hands for three years, refusing to intervene on behalf of the U.N., while the Serbs systematically decimated the Bosnian Muslim population; men, women and children armed with shotguns and pitchforks. What the West acquiesced to during the War in Bosnia made the My Lai Massacre in Vietnam look like child's play.

Diving from a tree in a park in Bosnia, 1996.

Friendly farm cat that Angela and I met on a hike in Switzerland, 1994.

want to be actors, that's *their* business. If they want to be *good* actors, that's also their business, but it's not the business of the people who control the film industry, the ones who tell the actors and the actresses and the directors and the writers and the cameramen, and all the rest of us into the bargain, what can and can't be seen on the silver screen.

These people, whoever they are (Brad Pitt knows who they are; so does River Phoenix.), have their own idea of what's *kosher* and what isn't, what's good for an actor's career and what isn't. What they don't have is any intention of letting their *protégés* become character actors—actors with character—for the simple reason that they're not in the business of promoting character, least of all Christian character.

The Devil sure as Hell isn't. He's out to destroy character any way he can, and I doubt if there's a more effective, persuasive way of doing that than through the medium of cinematography. That's my opinion, for what it's worth. I think the people who trade their God-given looks and talent for the kind of immortality that Hollywood offers are bought with a price (1 Corinthians 6: 20), just like we are, and their lives either glorify Hollywood and the gods of Hollywood or they don't work.

I'm glad they do work. I've seen *A River Runs Through It* twice and I'd see it again if I didn't have to wade through the anti-Christ bullshit that runs through it. Apart from the fishing, which is merely fictitious, it's a weak story with weak characters, two brothers whose favorite epithet is "Jesus Christ!" I don't believe that two preacher's sons from that era (early 1900s, rural Montana) would talk that way. I think somebody from *this* era, somebody from Hollywood with an axe to grind, *wanted* them to talk that way. Of course you can't do that—grind your anti-Christ axes in public—without somebody to do your dirty work for you, which is why I don't think much of the acting profession.

But that's just me talking and I've said enough. Before I go on to something else and before I'll let anybody tell me that I'm being too hard on Hollywood, here's something that Maria came out with recently.

Asked to name some of her personal dislikes, she put "bad movies" at the top of the list.

"I don't think people always realize just how powerful an influence movies have on them, even subconsciously. It really bothers me when people watch bad movies, because I know it's corrupting their spirits and hurting them, even if they don't realize it." (Ask Mama!—No.4 [#3281])

Sounds pretty bad to me, coming from Maria; that is, if she means to be taken literally. I don't have it in writing anywhere that that's the way she means to be taken, but I'd be surprised if she likes being "interpreted" any better than Dad did. I would be even more surprised if there was anything that she or Peter could do about it without becoming dictators.

Even Dad, as persuasive as he could be, couldn't do much about the decisions we were making. He could plead with us, which he often did; he could exhort with all longsuffering and doctrine (2 Timothy 4:2), which he often did; he could warn us of the consequences of our decisions; but he couldn't get us to think for ourselves with the mind of Christ.

If we were to find out today that the folks have had enough, that *we* have had enough of Hollywood to last the rest of our natural-born days, it wouldn't surprise me, but I would have to admit to a certain disappointment. Like all adult Family members I get one day off a week. When that blessed event arrives, there's nothing I like better than to kick back and be entertained.

Sometimes, when the stars are right and the script is right and the powers behind the scenes are willing to let their *proteges* step into the roles that God has gifted them to play, Hollywood can do a good deal better than that. It doesn't do it very often but often enough to suit me; often enough to make me wonder, with all the good movies there are to choose from—intelligently made, uplifting movies—why so few of them manage to survive the electoral process in our homes. This is not only democracy at its worst, it doesn't even do Hollywood justice.

I agree with Maria. I don't like it when the only thing good about the movie is the popcorn, and I don't like seeing a precious gift of God like discernment, which Dad said was one of the most important, needed gifts, treated like a disease.

★ *The Grapevine* was an in-house Family publication that featured testimonies from around the world, also film reviews. These reviews were not unlike the ones the Catholic Legion of Decency used to publish in the newspaper back in the '50s. Films were rated according to their "moral content": (A), "Morally Unobjectionable," (B), "Morally Objectionable in Part," or (C), "Condemned by the Legion of Decency."

A mortal sin was waiting for any Catholic who went to see a Condemned film. One such film that that I remember hearing about during that era was *The Moon Is Blue*. Anything that was considered mortally sinful in those days was also something that was likely to give you an erection, so we all knew what was wrong with *The Moon Is Blue*.

We could watch just about anything else: *Frankenstein*, *The Creature From the Black Lagoon*, *Psycho*, even if they gave you nightmares.

If you Google "Catholic Legion of Decency" you will see, interestingly enough, that Hollywood producers, forced to choose between artistic integrity and punishment at the box office, would delete certain morally offensive scenes from a film in order to gain the Church's indulgence, resulting in an upgrade from "Condemned" to "Morally Objectionable in Part," opening the coffers to millions of Catholic moviegoers with their millions of Catholic dollars.

With regard to nudity and/or the portrayal of a heated sexual encounter between consenting adults, the Family's approach to Hollywood was probably more lenient than either the Catholics or the Protestants, who held to the traditional Christian belief that sex, for it to have any propriety in the eyes of God, had to be licensed and controlled by the state, approved by the Church, and of course kept out of the public eye.

God Himself, according to this scenario—in contrast with the scriptural scenario, "Neither is there any creature that is not manifest in His sight: but all things are naked and opened unto the eyes of Him with whom we have to do." (Hebrews 4:13)—couldn't bear to watch while we were humping away!—but was forced to tolerate it for procreational purposes, as opposed to recreational purposes.

What we objected to in the Family and fought to keep out of our homes had nothing to do with either recreational or procreational sex and everything to do with the anti-Christ themes and the blatantly anti-Christ language that pervaded most Hollywood productions. Filmdom, with its phalanx of artistic and technological wizardry, production budgets that rivalled the defense budgets of small nations, legions of handsome young men and women ready, willing and eager to say and do whatever

stardom might require of them, could rightly be called the *de facto* propaganda arm of the state.

If you wanted to know who the next war would be fought against,
who the good guys were (always Americans, British or Israelis), and who
were the bad guys (always Russians, Arabs, sometimes the French or the
Germans), all you had to do was show up for the latest big-screen block-
buster. The gospel according to Hollywood was the prelude—prophetic,
as it were—of the bunker-busting, village-destroying, faith-destroying wars
that were soon to follow, always in somebody else's backyard, never
America's or Britain's or Israel's.

On the home front, Hollywood was every bit as effective in molding
and manipulating America's social consciousness as she was in beating the
war drums. If you wanted to know who or what was about to pop up
next out of the cultural closet, Hollywood had the answers. (It can be
argued, as the Europeans have, that Hollywood is what the Americans
have in *place* of a culture, in the absence of any real culture, that all of
America's cultural eggs are being hatched inside a movie studio.)

When I became a regular moviegoer myself back in the '50s,
Hollywood's best-known leading men—Rock Hudson, Cary Grant,
Montgomery Clift, James Dean—were already solidly in the Sodomite
camp, useless to the women who adored them. This may have been common knowledge in L. A. or San Francisco, which were already havens for
the emerging Sodomite culture, but if you lived in rural California like I
did, it was hard to imagine Hollywood's male heartthrobs being anything
but *bona fide* ladies' men.

Defenders of the acting profession would no doubt argue that filmdom's
pan-sexual view of the world is merely a *reflection* of the culture at large,
a mirror but not the conduit for social behavior. Her legion of paying
customers would no doubt agree with this assessment, the alternative
being to admit that they have been successfully brainwashed.

To give credit where credit is due, the Catholics and religious Jews have
been and probably still are less susceptible to the machinations of the film
world than the Protestants have been, probably one of the reasons that so
many Catholics and Jews came to the Family in the early days.
Obedience to a central authority—the papacy or the rather exclusive

culture that many Jews grow up in—perhaps made it easier for us to recognize that what was coming to us out of Hollywood was neither *kosher*
nor edifying, nor even very interesting much of the time.

Like the Catholics and religious Jews, we rejected birth control and
abortion, which were not only sending millions of wannabe babies to the
garbage bin, it relegated women to the role of sex object, useful to *homo
erectus* for one thing.

Like everything else we preached, we practiced it. In less than two
decades our ranks had begun to swell from within, with families of six or
eight or 10 children becoming commonplace. First-generation adults were
beginning to be outnumbered by their offspring, now teens and young
adults, with eyes and ears of their own and minds of their own, including
the right to vote on video night.

As a New Religious Movement with high hopes for the future, our
future and the future of our children, we may have been naïve in expecting
them to follow dutifully in our footsteps. This was ignoring our own
experience, most of us having spent decades in the hog trough before we
were willing to admit to ourselves that God might have something better
for us than our parents did. We might have been smarter to do what the
Amish did with their kids and kicked them out of the nest when they
turned 18, not letting them back in again until they were old enough and
wise enough to decide for themselves what mattered to them and what
didn't.

While it would be unfair to blame Hollywood for the dissolution of
the Family, it would be deaf, dumb and blind to the facts to deny that the
overall behavior of at least two generations of Family young people was
corrupted, at least in part, by the entertainment industry, which included
not only Hollywood but the music world.

The vocabulary of our teens, their manner of dress, their outward af-
fections and loyalties, their free-time activities, the influence they had on
their younger brothers and sisters, were too close to what was coming to
them via the silver screen and their headphones for us to ignore that Hollywood and rock & roll had become powerfully negative influences in
their lives.

Living communally, as it turned out, turned out to be the least challenging aspect of life on the mission field. Little has been written about this aspect of first-century Christianity apart from Luke's treatment in the Book of Acts, which doesn't go into much detail about it, probably because the way they were living didn't matter as much to them as the message they were given to preach. But much can be gleaned from a literal, common-sense approach to the second and fourth chapters, as opposed to the modern, apologetic approach, which supposes that the practice of communal living was flawed from the beginning, doomed to die a natural death.

Suffice it to say that few modern Christians have dipped their toes in the communal waters.

CHAPTER NINE:

A DISEASE CALLED DISCERNMENT

That's what they treated it like in college, too, a disease, an obnoxious religious disease, and the only cure for it was to pretend you didn't have it. To do that you had to pretend, of course, that what we were reading didn't mean literally what it was saying, because if you were to take most of what we were reading literally, seriously, it didn't make any sense. But that was OK. Making sense, after all, was not the point of a higher education.

Making money now, that made sense, and a lot of my professors were making a lot of money by not making a lick of sense, including the money they were getting from the publishing companies for the books they were pushing onto the students, books that few of us would have been caught dead reading, much less buying, under any other circumstances. (Buying the books was supposed to give us the impetus to read them, the academic equivalent of getting your money's worth.)

I had some good professors though, men and women for whom teaching was more than a paycheck. One of them, Dr. Robert O'Neill, was from my mother's home state of Montana. (My father was born in Wyoming. That's two of the best trout-fishing states in North America, by the way.) An avid trout fisherman himself, Dr. O'Neill showed me how to tie a fly that he claimed was his own creation, drew it for me on a piece of paper, a dry fly that I came to use almost exclusively before I joined the Family. Tied on size 12 hook, or a size 10 for late-evening fishing, with yellow floss for the body, deer hair for the tail (or golden pheasant tippet if you wanted it to look pretty); two hackles, one grizzly and one brown, and deer hair for the wings; it's a real standup fly that killed a lot of fish for me. Nowadays I use simpler tackle.

Dr. O'Neill taught a class called *Writing of Rhetoric*, a three-unit course that met twice a week, and once a week each of the students had to meet with him in his office to discuss what we had written. During one of these meetings Dr. O'Neill ("Call me Bob."), knowing of my fondness for Hemingway, sent me to the library with another piece of paper, to the Periodicals section, to look for a magazine that I had never heard of before—*The Paris Review*—a literary magazine that featured interviews with some of the famous writers, including Hemingway.

It was one of the few times the famous American had allowed himself to be interviewed, and I was very keen to hear what he had to say.

CHAPTER 10:

HIGHER THAN WHAT?

A whole generation of critics had grown up around Hemingway, including most of my professors in the English Department. Educated in some of the best American universities, most of them Ph.D.'s, they regarded Hemingway as one of their patients, one who suffered from a disease known as *machismo*, a highly-contagious social disease peculiar to men, in fact exclusive to men, those with a *penchant* for food and drink, extramarital sex, hunting, fishing, boxing, bullfighting, and other unwholesome activities.

When he was 18, the age of a college freshman, Hemingway was driving ambulances on the Italian front under the bombardment of Austrian artillery. This was 1918. America had just entered the Great War, as it was called, Great because of the great number of people it killed. Over the next four decades he became the best-known, and some would say the most important, literary figure of the 20th Century, winning the Pulitzer Prize and the Nobel Prize for Literature in 1953 and 1954, all of this without the dubious benefits of a "higher" education.

He despised the *literati* as he did the press. They were all *remora*, he said, scavenger fish that attach themselves to sharks, or they were hyenas and jackals, low-level predators that profit from the hard work and muscle of real killers. He died in 1961, shot himself in what one of my professors described as "a final act of machismo."

That was 1961, a year before Marilyn Monroe, two years before Kennedy. America was losing her idols one by one.

CHAPTER 11:

THE INGERSOLL WATCH

I remember at least two things from this interview, one of them having to do with the gift of discernment. George Plimpton, editor-in-chief of the magazine, was conducting the interview, asking the kinds of questions you'd expect him to be asking.

He wanted to know what he secret was. What was it about Hemingway's "distinctive prose" that made it so distinctive? What was it that a writer needed most? If there was one single ingredient that a serious writer could not do without, what would it be?

Hemingway's answer—"A built-in shit detector."—may not have been what Plimpton was wanting to hear, but it was exactly what I wanted to hear, what the kid sitting in the front row of the church wanted to hear when the preacher offered him the watch.★ Hemingway was the preacher and I wanted that watch!—not only because of who it belonged to but I had the feeling it was something I was going to be needing in my own life. I was right about that. If ever anybody needed a shit detector, it was me. I'm pretty sure that I didn't ask God for it. The word "discernment" was not in my vocabulary at the time, and I couldn't very well have asked in faith, as a Catholic accustomed to praying to the Virgin Mary, for a good shit detector, but I believe that's what I got.

Some theological hairsplitters might disagree with me on this, but I'm satisfied that a good shit detector works just as well and is just as pleasing in the sight of God as the kind that Paul was talking about in Hebrews (4:12; 5:12-14).

It's the gift of God, "not of works, lest any man should boast" (Ephesians 2:9), given to those who want it and need it, not necessarily to those who think they have a right to it religiously, or because their parents have it, any more than salvation belongs to the Jews just because they're Jews.

Unfortunately for me, my own gift wasn't good enough to keep me out of the Army, and while I was in there I probably used it in ways that weren't very good for me spiritually. For one thing, it was not a gift that I even remotely associated with God anymore, if I ever had. If anything I was using it to protect myself from the very things that I did associate with God, such as the Army, the government, the Catholic Church, etc.

I didn't have a clue what was going on in my own life, needless to say. If somebody had told me then that God was the one who was trying to get me to think for myself, or that Jesus Christ, the Son of God, was behind my anti-war sentiments, I don't think I would have done him the courtesy of laughing in his face. I was getting dumber by the minute but my "gift," such as it was, may have kept me out of even worse trouble, the kind that landed me in the Army in the first place. It didn't keep me from getting sent to Vietnam but at least I got to go on my own terms.

★One of our leading evangelists one evening, in desperation, trying to explain the principle of faith, offered an Ingersoll watch he held in his hand to the largest of a group of boys sitting on the front seat of the church.

"Sonny, would you like to have this watch?" said the evangelist, holding it out to him.

"Aw, go 'long," answered the little fellow. "You can't fool me."

Looking at the next lad, the evangelist repeated the question. Quickly there came the answer, "Whatcha think I am?" This ain't any April Fool."

Again the question was repeated, and again and again down the line came similar jocular answers. At last the evangelist offered the watch to a little fellow about five years old, who was sitting on the edge of his seat, with bright, eager eyes, focused intently on the face of the speaker. His little feet did not touch the floor, but he was balanced on the edge of the seat just ready to leap, and the evangelist did not even have the opportunity of finishing his sentence, which he began on this wise: "Little man, would you like..." That was enough, for the chubby hand quickly grabbed the watch. Grabbed is the only word to describe the intense, eager action of the believing child, who instantly pocketed the gift, and while wiggling back on the seat in a pleased manner, said with a satisfied, grown-up sigh, that it was just what he had been wanting all the time.

After the service, the crowd of boys surrounded the evangelist with protests. "Aw, g'wan, how'd a feller know you really meant it?" and "Say, that's jus' the kind of watch I was wanting."

"Why didn't you tell us you were in earnest?" and then another. "If you really meant it, why didn't you put it in my hand, or say it to me again, so's I'd know."—Virginia Brandt Berg

CHAPTER 12:

A COMPELLING ARGUMENT

Going to Vietnam on my own terms—telling the Army to go to Hell *before* they put me on the plane, as opposed to waiting until I got back, if I got back, and then developing a conscience about it—may not have been the smartest thing I ever did. If I had kept my mouth shut I wouldn't have had to go at all.★

But sending me to Vietnam was never the worst thing they could do to me in the Army; neither was keeping my mouth shut the smartest thing I could have done to stay out of trouble. I was already in trouble and so was everybody else.

Not everybody looked at it this way, of course. My classmates in Special Forces, for example, they too were going to Vietnam on their own terms; untroubled, as it were, by the voice of conscience. We were medics, that was their conscience. Our mission and purpose in Vietnam, they argued, was to rescue fallen comrades, not to see how many gooks we could kill.

Our job description, our Military Occupational Specialty, set us apart, morally and intellectually, from the yahoos in Small Arms and Demolitions, or the cloak-and-dagger boys in Intel.

It was a compelling argument, especially if you believed it. What kept me and a couple other guys in this class from believing that we were the

Florence Nightingales of the John Wayne Brigade was knowing how disappointed our diehard brethren would be if the war should end prematurely, before they had the chance to distinguish themselves on the field of battle—rescuing fallen comrades—proving their hard-won medical prowess. In this they were no different from the yahoos in Small Arms and Demolitions or the cloak-and-dagger boys in Intel. A piece of the action is what they had signed up for. A piece of the action is what they would get.

It's what I had signed up for, too, only to discover, sooner rather than later, that I had been deceived, by the war machine and by my own good intentions.

"There is a way which seemeth right unto a man, but the end thereof are the ways of death." (Proverbs 14: 12)

These ways of death had seemed so right to me for so long that I could understand somebody wanting to go off to war, gung-ho to get his gun off—or gung-ho to stop the bleeding— only to find out when he gets back, if he gets back, his fingers burned and bloodied, that his conscience is right there where he'd left it.

I can understand somebody like General Smedley Butler, one of America's most decorated heroes, saying, after 33 years in the Marine Corps, that in all those years he had not had *a single original thought*. I can imagine him saying that. I have a harder time believing it!— not because I doubt the general's sincerity, or because my own three years in the Army (two years as a buck private) makes me an authority on the military mind; only because the life of a soldier, for me and a couple other guys I knew, turned out to be nothing if not fertile ground for originality. I never had a single original thought *until* I became a soldier.

That original thought, that split second behind the barracks at Fort Lewis, my first unexpurgated glimpse of America the Beautiful—with her pants down and her guns loaded—cured me of my patriotism in a flash. After that there was nothing to stop me from listening to my conscience. The only thing standing in my way now was the Church.

*My medics class returned to Fort Bragg in August of '69 after six months of Phase II training and a month of OJT, ready to begin preparations for the orals exam and graduation. This was when we began hearing that the Army had been cranking out too many Green Berets for the number of slots that needed to be filled in Vietnam.

Fully-trained, newly-graduated Small Arms and Demolitions Specialists were being put to work in the motor pool at Fort Bragg, or placed on endless maneuvers. A medic wanted to go to Vietnam badly enough—and everybody in my class except for Golden and me wanted to go badly enough—had to put his name on a list and get approval from higher up.

Fortunately for my classmates, Staff Sergeant Jim Slough and Spec Five Merton Tiffany were already battle-savvy medics when they came to Special Forces, both of them well-respected, well-decorated lifers. Their recommendations were enough to get the entire class to Vietnam, minus Golden and myself.

CHAPTER 13:

THE OPIATE OF THE MASSES

When Marx called religion the opiate of the masses, he was talking about people like me, good little churchgoers like I was. From the time I started attending mass regularly, under the penalty of mortal sin, from the age of seven, the age of accountability for Catholics, to the time I finally stopped going in the Army when I was 23, I can remember missing *twice*; once in grammar school when I was sick (my mother had to call the rectory to find out if my temperature was high enough) and once in college when I couldn't find the church.

Sixteen years of relentless churchgoing did not make me an exemplary Catholic, not where I came from. All it did was keep me from going to Hell for that particular mortal sin. (One was all it took.) But I was never a *troublesome* Catholic, as God is my witness. If I could have told the Army to go to Hell without locking horns with the Church, I would have. But I would have needed somebody to explain a few things to me first. For starters, I would have needed to know how and why and where and when "the One True Church Instituted by Christ to Give Grace"—her definition of herself in the Catechism—had become an agent of the United States Government! By whose authority?

Because only a decade earlier, in grammar school, when I was getting straight A's in Religion, the nuns had made it very clear to us that we Catholics belonged to God and not the government! Church teaching *vis-à-vis* the Separation of the Church and State was no different, in fact, from that of the founding fathers of the Constitution, whose original intent had been to protect the Church *from the State*, and not the reverse.

We were Catholics first, Americans second... I forget what we were after that. Republicans! But whatever we were, in matters of faith and morals we kowtowed to nobody, not to the president, not to the government, not to the politicians who ran it. When it came to the crunch, only the Pope, the Vicar of Christ on Earth, could tell us what to do.

What the Pope was telling me to do now—if I was to believe what the chaplain was telling us!—was to keep my Catholic mouth shut. My patriotic duty had now become my religious duty.

Voila!

I thought about writing him a letter (Pope Paul VI), letting him know what was going on behind his back. Surely if he, the Vicar of Christ on Earth, knew what these priestly scoundrels were up to, surely he would step in and do something about it! Because doing something about it is what the Catholic religion was all about! The nuns and the Christian Brothers always "did something about it" when any of us got out of line. My father always "did something about it," and not only when his own family was involved.

Once in my early teens, returning from a weekend in San Francisco, where my brother Richard was now living and working, tending bar at La Rocca's Corner on Columbus Avenue, as we approached the driveway at 1604 North Middleton Street in Hanford, there to greet us, the front end partway under the carport, the back end hanging out over the curb, was a brand-new boat-and-trailer!—a nice long white and blue one with a windshield and a steering wheel and a big Evinrude motor sticking up in back.

Before I could say "FISHING!" or my brother Gary could say "WATER-SKIING!" my father muttered, "That sonofabitch!" And we all knew that this was the last any of us would see of our new boat.

"That sonofabitch," one of my father's customers from the bank, was in for it.

Without another word he parked the car and went to the sliding glass door at the side of the house, opened it with his keys and marched to the phone. For the next few minutes my mother and Gary and I waited in the backyard under the fruitless mulberry, listening to the *oratorio*, not daring to go inside until he was finished, happy that somebody else was getting it for a change. My father's passion for the English language (he studied the dictionary the way some people do the Bible), and his fondness for certain expressions in the American idiom, rolled off his tongue, on occasions like these, like lava down the slopes of a volcano.

He lived by the Old Testament dictum, "Because sentence against an evil work is not executed speedily, therefore the heart of the sons of men is fully set in them to do evil." (Ecclesiastes 8: 11)

He also lived by the New Testament dictum, "Whoso keepeth his word, in him verily is the love of God perfected." (1John 2: 5)

He could be a hard man to live with when his temper got the better of him—unpredictable—but if he told you he was going to do something, for better or for worse, you could bank on it. And he was generous to a fault with his own money, handing out five-dollar tips to waitresses back in the day when they were lucky to get a quarter. And he sent "my son the Protestant," as he took to calling me after I joined the Family, to the mission field in 1986.

But when it came to the bank's money or somebody else's money, he refused to budge, not when the lady at the Safeway checkout gave him too much change, not when the sonofabitches of this world tried to bribe him.

CHAPTER 14:

THE ONE TRUE CHURCH

Another Catholic who dazzled me—dazzled my father also—with his forthrightness and his elocution was Monsignor Thomas J. Earley,★ pastor at Sacred Heart Parish in Salinas while I was growing up.

My father made it a point to attend Father Earley's masses, not only because he was a great admirer of the Monsignor, paying him the highest earthly compliment he could think of ("He would have made a wonderful executive!"), but because he could say an entire mass, including the sermon, in 20 minutes.

One Sunday while the Monsignor was engaged in the *Prayers at the Foot of the Altar* (This is the back-and-forth exchange between the celebrant and the servers at the very beginning of the mass, before the priest ascends the steps for the *Offertory*.), there arose a commotion behind him, the sound of footsteps.

A business associate of my father's, one of the wealthiest members of the congregation, was tip-toeing up the center aisle with his wife and kids, leading them to their accustomed pew at the front of the church, a bench-and-padded-kneeler that he had paid for many times over with his generous contributions to the Sacred Heart Building Fund.

Two minutes late!

Turning and beholding the fellow, Father Earley thundered, "How *dare* you come in here like this, disrupting the mass!? Go stand in the back with the rest of the latecomers!"

And the poor fellow turned, gathering his humiliated wife and kids together before the entire congregation, and did as he was told. Because God had spoken. Because Monsignor Earley, although he murdered the Latin, never murdered the truth.

I thought of him often during those murderous years in the Army. He was the closest thing to Jesus that I had ever seen in the Catholic religion, the kind of Jesus I was looking for: not the Romanized, Italianized, limp-wristed Son of Mary, but the valiant Son of Man who went about everywhere doing good, "doing something about it," such as whipping the hirelings who called themselves priests out of the temple.

The Pope that I believed in would have gone even further, making it an excommunicable offense for any Catholic of any nationality to participate in the war in any way, shape or uniform.

END OF WAR! PEACE ON EARTH! GOOD WILL TOWARDS MEN OF GOOD WILL!

The Protestants, of course, would have to follow suit, not to be outdone by the idol-worshippers. They could make it sound like it was their own idea for all I cared!—but let them fight the God-damned war without the Catholics! Let them get somebody else to rouse the troops! Let the bloody politicians do it! Let *them* see if they could persuade anybody that God was on their side! Let the arms manufacturers do it!

"Give us your sons and we'll give you a twenty bucks for every gook they kill!"

My sympathies were on the side of the Church to the bitter end. By the time I was ready to admit to myself that there had to be something rotten in Rome for it to stink so bad in North Carolina, it was obvious, even to me, that the stench did not emanate solely from the Vatican; not much consolation to me at the time, or much of a surprise. If I learned anything at all in my miserable three years in the Army, it was that the Military/Industrial Complex was nothing if not a RELIGIOUS complex. They were all in on it, every last one of them, every chaplain I ever listened to, every denomination. They were all on the bandwagon, doing it for Uncle Sam.

*Father Earley lost 20 feet of his intestines to cancer while I was going to Sacred Heart.   With everybody praying for him, offering up rosaries and masses and Novenas, doing what devout Catholics do when they want God to perform a miracle for them, a few months later he was back on the job. His customarily short masses were taking a little longer now because swallowing the host and the wine during the *Offertory* was difficult for him, and it was hard for him to talk, but his sermons had lost none of their pithiness or their good humor.

The resurrection of Father Earley was the only Catholic miracle that I was ever a party to personally. He ended up marrying his housekeeper and longtime sweetheart and lived to a ripe old age, a Catholic success story if I ever heard one.

CHAPTER 15:

MATTHEW, MARK LUKE AND JOHN

Since nobody was going to do anything about it, least of all the Pope, and with nobody to tell me what to do about it, except for the Pope, I had to decide whether to go along with the Church in her military/industrial whoredoms or, as so often happens when religion and conscience don't mix, become a heretic.

I went along with it for seven months, marching off to the chapel every week on four different Army bases, trying hard not to notice that the message I was getting every Sunday from the chaplains—ordained priests who spoke and acted under the auspices and direction and foreknowledge of the Church—was the same pure unadulterated horseshit that the Army was feeding us during the week.

There were two ways I could have looked at it. Either the Church was getting it from the Army or the Army was getting it from the Church. Either way it was nasty business, the worst kind of nasty business, the kind that makes the average street hooker look like a charity worker. It's the kind of religious whoredom that Jesus rakes over the coals in the 17th and 18th chapters of Revelation; the kind that makes Him want to puke in the 3rd chapter.   But I'm getting ahead of myself. I'm starting to sound like a Protestant when I haven't finished being a Catholic yet!—

quoting scripture before I've even read it.

It would be another six long years before I would begin to see for myself, in Matthew, Mark, Luke and John, how slight was the resemblance between the Christ of the Catholics and the one who graces the scripture. It was worth the wait. As books go, the Bible turned out to be everything that one of my Jewish professors said it would be.

In my junior year at Fresno State I took a class called *World Literature*. It was one of the course requirements for a liberal arts major. During one of these classes a student began making some unscholarly pronouncements about a book that we were supposed to have read. This fellow was an upper-classman and an English major and should have known better, but he couldn't say enough about this book, this "important" work of English fiction.

Clearly, he said, such-and-such by so-and-so stood alone in the annals of classical English literature.

Dr. Bluestein (Eugene) sang and played banjo in a bluegrass band with other faculty members. He waited until the hole that this fellow was digging for himself was too deep to get out of without professional help; then he cleared his throat and lifted a finger.

"In a purely literary sense" he began, "the King James Version of the Bible is *perhaps the finest, most enduring work of prose and poetry in the English language…*"

This remark, uttered out of the blue by a Jewish intellectual, startled me to my Catholic roots. It was the first time that anybody in authority— and Dr. Bluestein was nothing if not an authority on English literature— had suggested in my hearing that the Bible could be anything but a book of Protestant doctrine; inspired, no doubt, by Martin Lucifer himself.

According to the nuns, not even they or the line-level priesthood were supposed to be reading it. There was scripture within the Catholic liturgy—John Chapter One, for example—and that was OK because it was part of the Mass, safely wrapped in the arms of Our Holy Mother the Church; but only the "Church Fathers"—Church appointed theologians—could be trusted with an extemporaneous reading of this dangerous book. They were the only ones who wouldn't get *the wrong impression*, like Martin Lucifer did.

I ended up getting the wrong impression anyway, without any help from the Bible, without becoming a Protestant, and without falling prey to any of the non-Catholic teachings of Jesus Christ except for the ones that I was getting directly from the chaplains, along with plenty of corroborating testimony from their henchmen in the military.

I didn't know the Whore that rides the back of the Beast (Revelation 17: 5) from Annie Oakley!—but I knew what she did for a living, and whom she did it with, and whom she did it to, and whom she vilified and condemned and consigned to the fires of Hell for daring to lift up a voice against her.

I knew that organized religion, led by the Catholics and followed dutifully by her Protestant daughters, was working hand-in-glove with the war machine, absolutely indispensable to the smooth running of the war machine; holding the reins—like Annie Oakley—telling the Beast which way to turn, whom to trample and whom to vindicate, whom to wage war upon and whom to welcome into the fold.

I knew there was something singularly rotten in America and that somebody, or maybe a lot of somebodies, were doing their damnedest to keep it that way. What I didn't know, what I was never able to fathom until Dad came along and spelled it out for me, finally, three years after I got out of the Army; what never entered my Catholic head until the moment of my salvation was that the Church, no matter how powerful she is, no matter how persuasive she can be, no matter how ruthlessly she defends her image before the faithful—"teaching for doctrines the commandments of men" (Mark 7: 7)—can't stop God from speaking to His children, even when they don't know that they're His children, even when they can't believe that He could be speaking to them, through the voice of conscience, telling them something that's completely contrary to what the Church is telling them.

What that voice was telling me—without the Church's permission—was that the gospel according to the war machine was one unholy crock of shit and that I wasn't much of a man or much of a soldier or even much of a Catholic if I kept on listening to it.

CHAPTER 16:

MEN WITHOUT WOMEN

Without an inkling that God could be involved or even interested in the decisions I was making, it naturally never occurred to me that my thoughts could be His thoughts or that the path I was on could be leading me anyplace but straight to Hell. It led straight to Fort Bragg where, for the next year and a half (including the six months I was on the boxing team and the seven months I was TDY at Fort Sam and Fort Polk), Uncle Sam gave us plenty to think about besides the fate of our immortal souls.

Saying my goodbyes to the God of the Catholics turned out to be the easiest thing I ever did in the Army. From one week to the next I went from being the only trainee in the brigade who went to mass every Sunday—23 years old and still an altar boy—to just another trainee who did what every other trainee was doing every Sunday, sleeping in until 8 o'clock with the rest of the herd. Nothing else had changed. I had gained nothing but an hour or two of sleep and lost nothing but my religious conceit, but it was enough to make me, for the first time in my life, a tough guy in good standing. This allowed me to observe, at close range, what makes a tough guy tick.

What makes a tough guy tick is horniness: prolonged periods of mental and physical duress in a strictly male, womanless environment. A good hardon, coupled with the urge to sing when the flag is being raised, makes a tough guy tick.

If soldiers were issued females the way we were issued everything else in the military; if God's first words to the human race (Genesis 1:28), and His last words to Noah after the Flood (Genesis 9:1), were as dutifully observed within the military as the laws of man are dutifully observed while the laws of God are dutifully ignored, it would sink the Republic. Because an army of sexually satisfied, sexually healthy young men with wives and children of their own would think twice before marching into somebody else's backyard, guns a-blazing, knowing, in a heartbeat, that the kind of murderous, asinine behavior that passes for manliness in the military—"men with men working that which is unseemly" (Romans 1: 27), as the apostle Paul puts it, referring to the ultimate expression of this particular form of masculine asininity—is sowing the seeds of your own destruction.★

Because no matter who was telling you to do it and no matter what awards or honors awaited you for doing it, you would still have to face your wife when you got back home. Such a woman, if she were up to federal standard—of she had half the guts that her husband was supposed to have—would be asking such questions as, "You did WHAT?..."

And then where would we be? Who would be afraid of us then? America's enemies would begin to see us as easy prey! Pussy-whipped! Soon they would be invading our shores! We might be forced to fight a war in our own backyard for a change!—perish the thought.

Or—and which is even unrighteous to consider, incomprehensible to the average dickheaded American—the rest of the world might begin to see us as a nation worth emulating after all, people to be followed rather than feared.

"Nevah happen," as Miss Bau★★ used to say to the GIs who wouldn't let her walk across the room without trying to get in her pants.

"Nevah happen."

God would never let it happen, the god of the Americans. The military/industrial god of the Americans would sooner sink the rest of the world than allow His own people, His chosen ones, to reap what they have sown.

*The Army that I belonged to for two years, 10 months and 22 days was a womanless institution. There was a regiment of WACs at Fort Sam while we were stationed there, with some mingling between the sexes on weekends (Randy Bream, one of my classmates in the medics program, ended up marrying a WAC.), but the military experience, stateside and in Vietnam, was anything but female-friendly.

Historically we know that there has never been an empire that did not regard women as detrimental to the fine art of single-minded soldiering. The ancient Greeks, we are told, took the direct approach to this dichotomy between the sexes by supplying soldiers with wives; only these "wives" were not women.

Whether these not-women were soldiers themselves, with their own MOS or Military Occupational Specialty (use your imagination here), or just male prostitutes brought in to service the troops, we don't know, but the practice is said to have made the Greek soldier invincible in battle, impervious to the debilitating influence of the female.

In America, up to and including the Vietnam era, male homosexuals were considered to be mentally, morally, medically and psychologically unfit to serve in the Armed Forces; medically because of the diseases they were known to carry and to transmit indiscriminately. The AIDs epidemic had already begun or was about to begin. Being a Sodomite (to use the biblical term) was a way to get out of the Vietnam draft if you could bring it off.

Nowadays, as I understand it, even a full-blown Sodomite cannot be excluded from military service solely on the basis of his sexual proclivities, his "orientation," as it is referred to nowadays in polite circles. (Political correctness is nothing if not political *politeness*.)

This idea, that what we are sexually has nothing to do with what we are as human beings, or what we are as soldiers, presented 50 years ago to a conference of psychologists or psychiatrists, would have been laughed off the stage. It would have started a civil war inside the military.

Nowadays?

Nothing changes but the language they use to describe themselves. A word that used to mean *joyous* or *lively, merry, happy, lighthearted, bright, brilliant* in most English dictionaries— often associated with springtime (or Christmas)—is now the verbal property of the Sodomites and the Sodomite sympathizers who use it like a bludgeon to evoke an act and a lifestyle that is the desecration of nature, of unregenerate man glorying in his own malodorous filth.

It is what it is. A Sodomite by any other name is still a Sodomite. (Isaiah 5: 20.)

If the end of all things is not at hand, it will be the first time in history that a nation obsessed with warfare and a military approach to the problems that beset mankind—always in somebody else's backyard—while ignoring every kind of deviltry in its own backyard, was not marching to its own defeat; the first time that public acquiescence in nonstop warfare and the acceptance of Sodomy as a legitimate form of sexual entertainment were not the terminal diseases that spelled the end of that nation, that empire, without exception.

As Billy Graham is said to have uttered once upon a time before he joined the circus in Washington, "If God doesn't destroy America, He will have to apologize to Sodom and Gomorrah."

★★Nguyen Thi Bau, civilian liaison for the 37th Signal Battalion, Da Nang Air Base, 1970.

CHAPTER 17:

JOHN THE FATHER

It turned out that *The Green Berets*, starring John Wayne, was an Army training film after all. I didn't find this out for sure until I got to Vietnam myself. I wasn't with the Green Berets anymore but John Wayne still was. If the Pentagon or whoever produced that film had any doubts about it being a hit when it hit the war zone, I'm here to tell them they needn't have doubted. The troops ate it up, much preferring it to the other two movies we had to choose from.

Sound of Music, starring Julie Andrews, was one of them. I think *Rio Bravo*, starring John Wayne, was the other one.

So it was the Duke on Saturday night, every Saturday night. On Sunday morning the chaplain would get up there. They showed the movies in the chapel, by the way. On the only night that I attended—my first Saturday as a member of the 37th Signal Battalion, Da Nang Air Base— the chaplain's assistant did the honors. One of his duties as a Conscientious Objector was bringing in the projector, mounting it on the podium and cranking it up, lighting up the wall of the vestibule with scenes from Warner Brothers. I had voted for Julie Andrews and went to bed.

The chapel was situated in the middle of the compound, next to the mail room and the photo lab, directly across from the Headquarters

Building, maybe 30 meters from where I slept, so I had to listen to that racket every Saturday night whether I wanted to or not.

"The rockets' red glare
The bombs bursting in air…"

…giving proof through the night that our flag with its bloody religion was still there, the religion that killed four of my friends that I know of (Looney, Wilson, Padgett, Robertson), not to mention the millions of other people's friends it killed and maimed and drove insane.

The chaplain, for his part, was just as good a bad actor as John Wayne was. I never heard him preach so I don't know how he came across religiously, but I heard him on other occasions, little pep talks that he would give the troops, so I think it's fair to say that the message he was giving them on Sunday was no different in substance or theology from the one that John Wayne was giving them on Saturday night.

"God is on our side! JOHN is on our side!"

I had a chaplain say these exact words to me, believe it or not. He wasn't kidding, either. He was the brigade chaplain, 1st Signal Brigade, a full colonel in the Army, which is pretty high up there for a priest. I doubt if he kidded very much about anything. He was a typical chaplain. I found them to be some of the most gung-ho, tight-assed, humorless people in the Army, real flag-wavers and Commie-haters, the kind of people the Army can't do without.

By this time I had become the kind of soldier they didn't know what to do *with*, which is why I had to see this character in the first place. First they send you to the chaplain, the man of God, to see if he can't talk some patriotic sense into you. Then they send you to the psychiatrist, the man of science, who turned out to be a lot more congenial about it than the chaplain was.

Oberti, his name was. I don't know if he was from the same olive-oil family that I knew in Fresno, California, but it was spelled the same way. This Oberti had the physique and personality of a fullback, not an olive grower. We sat across from each other at his desk at Brigade Headquarters.

I was allowed to ask questions. My first question was whether it was true that there were a lot of Catholics in Vietnam.

He grunted in the affirmative, drumming his beefy fingers on the desk.

So what happened, I asked him, when the planes were flying, over dropping their bombs? Some of these pilots had to be Catholics, right?—praying that God would save them and destroy the gooks. But some of the gooks on the ground were also Catholics, right?—praying that God would save them and destroy the Americans! Same God, same religion! Whose prayers does He answer?

BOOM! Father Fullback's fist came down on the desk. "God is on OUR side! And DON'T you forget it!

CHAPTER 18:

SURVIVAL OF THE FITTEST

I'm going back and forth here between Vietnam and the States. Now we're headed back to the States, back to the Green Berets. This is Phase I Training at Fort Bragg, sort of a boot camp for Green Berets. We're still wearing baseball hats.

With the heat and the sweat and the sunburned necks (August in North Carolina), my fellow fighting-age Americans were getting kicked out left and right for various minor but excommunicable offenses: late for formation, late for anything, complaining about anything, fainting, lying, crying, shooting your mouth off to the wrong people, smoking dope in the parking lot, etc. etc.

I may have had an especially strict upbringing—I don't think I did— but as the training progressed and the ranks began to dwindle, it became obvious that few of my fellow fighting-age Americans had had much discipline in their lives apart from what they were getting in the Army, and it was never enough to convince them that crime didn't pay. They were always looking around for some way to *make* it pay, and there was always somebody there watching them, waiting to clamp down when the mouse got too close to the cheese.

After three weeks of this, maybe a third of the original 180 would-be

John Waynes who had descended, like a plague, on Fort Bragg, had been terminated, or kicked out. You didn't get kicked out of Special Forces; you were "terminated." If you made it this far you were about average, I'd say. It was what you did the fourth and final week, the dreaded six days and nights they called Hell Week, that determined whether you were a true diehard or not or just stupid like I was.

As I said, I had no good reason for being in Special Forces in the first place. I certainly had no good reason for staying in except that I had already completed a fair amount of the training, so it behooved me to stick it out a little longer. I was already airborne-qualified, for one thing, which meant that if I were to quit now or get kicked out, I would be sent immediately to another airborne unit, either the 82nd at Fort Bragg—known as the Animal Farm—or more likely to the 101st in Vietnam, where they were presently catching Hell from the NVA; so it wouldn't have made much sense for me to all of a sudden do the "right" thing and quit.

The only right thing left for me to do in the Army was to tell Uncle Sam what I had been thinking since the first week of Basic. I owed him that much and I owed it to myself—and to my mother—to do it without getting myself killed or thrown in the stockade.

If I stayed in Special Forces the training would take me almost to the end of the first two years, then Vietnam. This would keep me usefully occupied while I waited for my path to become clear. Our principal instructor at Fort Sam told us we were getting the equivalent of two years of medical school, which might come in handy someday. And the longer I stayed in—the closer I came to graduating and becoming a full-fledged Special Forces medic—the more "reputable" I would become in the eyes of the lifers who judged me and everybody else, not by what we were thinking, but by our performance as soldiers.

So that's what I decided to do. When it came time to reveal my treasonous sentiments, Uncle Sam would have plenty to accuse me of, but he wouldn't be able to accuse me of insubordination or dereliction of duty or failure to cut the Special Forces mustard.

CHAPTER 19:

HELL WEEK

Hell Week began with a night jump somewhere over the boonies in North Carolina. It was the first time any of us had jumped at night and the first time with this much gear on our backs, 60 pounds worth: M-14s that weighed 10 pounds unloaded, sleeping bag, shelter half, entrenching tool, flashlight, full ration of C-rations, full canteen, complete change of fatigues and underwear, including fatigue jacket—in 90-degree North Carolina weather—towel, toothpaste, soap, shaving gear, etc. etc.

Back at the fort each of us had been given a list of everything we needed to bring for the next six days and nights, no more and no less. You get a lot of lists in the Army and this was one of them, one of the more important ones as it turned out. One of the things on this list was an extra pair of boots. We were wearing jungle boots, which are fairly light—a Hell of a lot lighter than what I ended up carrying in their place—but it seemed like a lot of unnecessary weight to be carrying around for six days, so I went around asking a few people about it the day we were packing in the barracks, and sure enough, I found a very knowledgeable PFC on the first floor assured me that I wouldn't need the extra boots.

"Why carry all that extra weight around?"

So I was about two *under*weight when I hit the ground that night.

After dumping our chutes, roll call and a casualty check, we were split up into groups. My group was presided over by two senior NCOs. One of them had a clipboard and a flashlight. The other guy was pushing a wheelbarrow. We were told to line up abreast, single file, two arm-lengths apart, and to take everything out of our rucksacks and spread it out on the ground in front of us.

They started on the left flank and worked their way down. When they got to me, the guy with the flashlight went through my stuff like he did everybody else's. Then he looked over at the guy with the wheelbarrow and shook his head and held up two fingers. The guy with the wheelbarrow reached in and pulled out two mortar dummies—concrete pineapples that weighed 15 pounds each—and proceeded to strap them onto the sides of my rucksack, one for each boot, a well-balanced load to help me remember what lists were for.

This extra 30 pounds of Ready-Mix became my constant companion for the next six days and nights. If I got caught taking one of them off— to sleep, to take a leak, to say my prayers—I was out, terminated. During those six days and nights I might have gotten two hours of uninterrupted sleep and ate one full ration of C-Rations, plus some crackers that I found on the ground and some berries that we weren't supposed to eat. Others may have gotten a little more, others a little less.

We were supposed to have gotten some goat meat, too, from six goats that were flown in for the occasion, dropped in on parachutes like the rest of us goats, live animals that we were supposed to have killed and butchered and eaten ourselves as part of the training, but I never saw any goat meat. The cadre probably got most of it and they definitely got all the beer.

I did see some snake meat over at the snake-eating exhibition. This turned out to be one of the highlights of my military career, just to warn you. This is what they refer to nowadays as a "bonding ritual" or "bonding episode." You get a lot of bonding episodes in the Army and this was one of them, one of the more impressive ones as it turned out. Usually they didn't amount to much. Usually you'd get two or three in the morning and another two or three in the afternoon, depending on what else we were doing. In the Army we called them cigarette breaks. ("Smoke'm if you got'm.")

While the troops were sucking on their Camels or their Luckies or their Marlboros, Old Sarge would slide into his routine: everything you never wanted to know about his sleazy sex life. If that didn't do it, if hearing what one of the greatest studs in military history had done to his old lady the night before, or his old lady's girlfriend; if that isn't enough to get you revved up and ready to rape, loot and pillage, you'd get a war story, automatic. After a while you couldn't tell the difference anymore between their sleazy sex lives and their sleazy military adventures; at least I couldn't. Technically there had to be some difference but it all sounded the same after a while: same story, same tactic, same objective, and basically the same enemy.

Charlie, for his part, was insatiable. He just kept coming at you— through the Claymores and the concertina, through the flamethrowers and the M-60s and the helicopter gunships— through everything Uncle Sam could throw at him. And of course the women kept coming too once old Sarge pulled out his six-shooter and went to work on them.

CHAPTER 20:

SNAKES AND PHALLIC SYMBOLS

That was the Marlboro treatment. Now we're getting the snake treatment. Everybody still with me? I hope all this symbolism isn't going over your heads. If it is, it's not because you weren't in the Green Berets like I was. It's because you didn't go to Catholic school like I did. Catholic school is where I got my sex education, in the fifth or sixth grade. Good old Sacred Heart is where I learned about snakes and phallic symbols.

It was either Sister Anna Theresa, my fifth-grade teacher (one of the Italian nuns), or Sister Marie Patrice, my sixth-grade teacher (one of the Irish nuns, four of whose brothers and sisters were nuns and priests, two of them Jesuits, one of them a bishop, the Bishop Hugh Donohoe), who gave us the lowdown on Adam and Eve, the inside scoop on the Fall of Man (the Fall of Woman), the beguilement of Eve in the Garden, her seduction by Satan, the loss of her virginity, along with the purity and innocence of mankind, to Lucifer the Arch-Penis.

That's not exactly the way she put it but that's the impression we were all supposed to get, that I got anyway. I can still picture him slithering across the front of the classroom, six feet long and headed straight for Sister Anna Theresa or Sister Marie Patrice!—old One-Eye himself.

According to this scenario dear Eve, the mother of us all, not only conspired with the Devil, she copulated with him, horror of horrors. This is pretty heavy stuff, with heavy implications for 11- or 12-year-olds. Catholicism, in its purest form, is a pretty heavy religion, which is one of the reasons I was never very susceptible to the kind of showmanship we were getting in the Green Berets. The Sisters of Notre Dame were a hard act to follow.

CHAPTER 21:

SNAKES AND CITY BOYS

The Army used real snakes though, I'll say that for them. The place was crawling with them, snakes and city boys, so they simply used the one to take advantage of the other, for which you could hardly blame the Army.

The instructor, for his part, was a fine specimen, six-and-a-half feet of bone and muscle, but it wasn't much of a snake. Copperheads don't get very big. They're not very poisonous, either, enough to kill a chicken or a rat, but they're about the right size with the right kind of poison for the kind of show they were trying to put on for us. Nothing like a little blood-and-guts to rev up the troops. God knows it didn't take much to get these guys revved up.

We were "at rest" now, with permission to move forward. ("At ease is a relaxed position, allowing some lateral movement, right foot in place. "Parade rest" is feet apart, eyes forward, hands clasped behind your back, no lateral movement and no talking. "At rest" is about as laid back as it gets during duty hours, a welcome relief from the tedium but dangerous at this point in our training.)

The wisecrackers from Wichita and Camden, New Jersey were beginning to throw caution to the winds.

"Hey, Sarge! You're outta uniform! Haw!"

Sarge is down to his T-shirt, so as not to get snakeshit on his fatigue jacket.

The star of the show is wrapped around his arm like a bracelet, below the 16-inch biceps, about to become the victim of oral decapitation.

"Better not get too close, Sarge! Your old lady might get jealous! Haw haw!"

Sarge is a little too busy just now to be messing with the city boys, but their comments do not go unnoticed. Nothing goes unnoticed. He's got as good a grip on the city boys as he does on the snake. Some of them won't be around much longer than the snake will, either. The eagle eyes on the perimeter will see to that. Already, in less than 24 hours, there are fewer mouths to feed, and fewer to listen to.

Because there are so many of us and so few of them, so few cadre to train us and keep us in line, this thinning of the ranks has become more than just an interesting sidelight to the training. For the cadre it's what they *do* 12 hours a day, six days a week.

At the end of all this, when it comes time to hand out the berets, they won't be handing out any more than they usually do. They won't be getting paid for it any more than they usually do, either, which is probably what makes them so irritable, having to babysit us when they could be doing something constructive with their lives, such as helping to stop the spread of Communism in Southeast Asia.

In civilian terms, this meant helping themselves to a good piece of the action while it lasted. Vietnam was what was known as a good "career war," the kind that goes on and on with no foreseeable end to the perks and benefits. For all the havoc it wrought in Vietnam, Laos and Cambodia; for all the farms and villages and virgin jungle it laid waste, for all the millions of men, women, children and livestock it tore limb-from-limb and burned to a stump; for all the Hell on earth it created 10,000 miles away, it paid for a lot of new houses back home and a lot of Corvette Stingrays, the vehicle-of-choice if you were a lifer in Special Forces. It was a lousy war if you happened to be married to one of these selfless individuals, or if one of them was your father, but hey! Glory has its price.

Apart from all this, apart from the purely mercenary aspects of war, or maybe because of it, my mentors at Fort Bragg were good at what they did. Life in the dead zone had given them the kind of insight into the dark side of human nature that made them, in the Darwinian sense, top-of-the-line people handlers, the best I've ever seen. I can still picture them moving through the ranks, always on the lookout for trouble, for any sign of mischief or discontent; for a grin where there shouldn't be one or any unsteadiness in the eyes; like farmers wading through the poultry pen, taking the sick ones out by the neck, giving them a quick twist and dropping them into the pig bucket—no muss, no fuss—so that the healthy ones hardly even notice.

More than just crowd pleasers and hatchet men, the Special Forces cadre were adept crowd manipulators, crowd controllers. *Mob control*, that's what it's all about. From boot camp to the Green Berets, that's what the men with the chevrons on their sleeves were experts at if they were experts at anything—mob control—and there's no better way to keep a mob under control, especially a mob of Americans, than by giving them something to kill for. Hence the snake, hence the war, hence everything else that goes on out there in the name of Christian civilization.

Social Darwinism? If that's what it is, if that's what you want to call it, it doesn't begin in the Army, believe me. It did for me because I didn't begin to recognize it until my nose was in it, with Uncle Sam's boot on my neck, but it wasn't the first time that somebody had taken advantage of my ignorance, or the first time that my lusts had been preyed upon, or the first time that somebody had tried to get me to think more highly of myself than I ought to think.

The schools do it too, so do the churches, and it does give them a meas-ure of control over you intellectually and spiritually, even physically for as long as they've got you, but this is where the Army takes its departure from the other brainwashing institutions. Especially during wartime when the stakes are higher and the ethical and legal restraints are fewer or nonexistent, when the pressure to conform is immeasurably greater, when other people's lives are at stake; the Army is in a league of its own and there's no referee.

Once they've got you they've *got* you, you belong to the government. You become a captive audience—*you* become the animals in the zoo—

and what they feed you, oftentimes, no matter what it is, no matter how ridiculous or nonsensical or unethical it is by any other standard, in the Army it goes down without a hitch, without a murmur of complaint or incredulity.

CHAPTER 22:

EXCEPTIONS TO THE RULE

Given the times and the mood of the country, one might have expected to find a number of exceptions to the above rule, even within the military, but I met only two, both of them in Special Forces. One of them was a kid from Indiana named Paul Wykes. A high school basketball star with a scholarship to Ball State University, he dropped out after one semester and went to Europe, where he played semi-pro ball with an English team. When he got back to the States in late '67, his draft notice was waiting for him.

Wykes was in my 91A (Basic Medics) class at Fort Bragg, a tall, blonde, friendly kid with the dangerous habit of laughing when he wasn't supposed to. After 91A I was on the boxing team for seven months. When I came back to Special Forces in the spring of '69, Wykes was in my 91B class (Advanced Medics) that was headed to Fort Sam (Houston) in San Antonio, Texas.

Our principal instructor at Fort Sam was a surgeon and a captain in the Army. His upbeat, rather diffident approach to the carnage that we were being trained to deal with brought out the worst in Wykes; or the best, depending on how you looked at it.

One day the doctor was showing us a series of slides, the medical history of an NCO who had taken an AK-47 round in the face. The tendency for the AK projectile to "tumble" when deflected by bone had removed most of the soft and cartilaginous tissue. Progressing through the slides, the doctor, a tall, slender, dark-haired fellow, gave a running commentary on the reconstruction process, culminating, in the final slide, with a line of suture marks that ran above and through one of the eyes, down and across where the nose and mouth had been, and ending under the chin on the other side.

He had obviously taught this class a number of times but none of us had seen a face like this. The show ended with him remarking rather breezily, "Of course we aren't finished with him yet."—Meaning our faceless comrade was in for further improvements.

Wykes, who had remained silent throughout the exposition, building up steam as it were, let out an explosive "*Pshewww!*" from the back of the room, followed by an expletive that he often used when he couldn't do the subject justice.

"Ree-DICK-you-luss!"

As ridiculous as it was, as utterly nonsensical as it was for us to suppose that we or any legion of medics was going to restore what the entire weight of the military establishment was hellbent on destroying; it was possible, if you had majored in journalism, to be objective about it. One had to admit that most cutting-edge surgical advances, particularly in the fields of plastic surgery, burn trauma and prosthetics, are tested and refined during war and because of war and as a direct consequence of war; what the arms manufacturers and even some within the medical establishment would point to as some of the collateral *benefits* of war.

Wykes wasn't around much longer. I was glad to see him go. So was everybody else. Unlike the others, I felt he deserved to get kicked out after trying so hard for so long to give Uncle Sam every opportunity to kick him out, facing the music rather than running from it. The rest of our class, the ever-dwindling number of A-Team candidates who wanted to get on with the show and onto the killing fields, would have argued that the music wasn't so bad once you got used to it.

By refusing to let the Army make a soldier out of him, refusing to attend class in the heat of summer when there was a swimming pool nearby, refusing to shine his boots (refusing to put anything on his boots but mink oil, which made it impossible to shine his boots); refusing to pull KP under any circumstances, keeping a sleeping bag stashed in the woods for these and other emergencies; by taking off twice to Canada to go moose hunting with his brother Phil; by pulling two stretches in the Fort Bragg Stockade, including a month in solitary; the ever-cheerful Wykes, one of two people I knew in the Army who never cussed, never lost his temper, was finally given his walking papers.

The last time I saw him at Fort Bragg he had his buckskin jacket on and was headed north, back to his beloved canoe trips and his Gordon Lightfoot albums.

CHAPTER 23:

THE OTHER EXCEPTION

The other exception was PFC Stuart Golden, Honor Graduate from Phase I and Phase II Training. Golden and I took 91B together at Fort Sam, followed by OJT (On-the-Job Training) at the hospital at Fort Polk, Louisiana. The Army training center for medics (Brooke Army Medical Center) was at Fort Sam. Fort Polk, with its torrid climate and swampy terrain, was the last stop for infantry on their way to Vietnam.

Fort Polk produced the only fatality I saw in the Army, and the worst casualty, both of them heat-related. The casualty was a fair-skinned toddler whose parents had left him in the sun too long. They brought him in one Saturday afternoon after a picnic at a nearby lake with second- and third-degree burns on his neck and shoulders. Stu and I were on duty, equipped with the latest: heavy, yellow, chemically-soaked pads developed in response to America's napalm warfare in Vietnam. We applied these to the boy's blistering neck and shoulders after conferring with the doctor on duty. We couldn't give him morphine because he was too young, and there was nothing we could give to the parents, a young southern couple barely out of high school. They stood there wringing their hands, listening to the screaming, saying over and over that somebody should have *told* them.

My first solo assignment as a medic also involved screaming children:

giving pre-toddlers their first shots. One of the senior medics led me to a room where a table loaded with bottles, cotton swabs and disposable syringes was laid out for me. Stretching from the table to the wall at the back of the clinic was a line of military mothers holding their little ones.

I can't remember what I was injecting them with or what it was supposed to protect them from, but there was no protecting them from me. The mothers were instructed to pull the diapers up as far as they would go and to present them to me one at a time, one chubby thigh at a time. Each little soldier would look me over fearlessly, blinking like chickens as I rubbed them with the antiseptic, never knowing what all the screaming was about until the needle went in.

If I had any desire to be a medic after my weeks in Emergency and Pediatrics, it was gone after my week on the Vietnam Ward. One of our patients was a buck sergeant, a door gunner who had taken two .50 caliber machine-gun rounds under the thigh; typical, according to the doctor who accompanied us on our rounds, of the "challenges" we would be facing "across the pond." The penicillin they were mainlining him wasn't doing the job, he told us. If he didn't start showing some dramatic improvement soon they were going to have to amputate at the hip.

His bed was up as high as it would go, his leg suspended from a pulley so we could get at it from underneath. He lay there each day spread-eagled, hooked to the IVs, never saying a word as we undid the bandages and went to work on the putrid mess, his black eyes burning holes in our clean white jackets, the clean white doctor giving a running commentary on the vagaries of .50-caliber machine-gun trauma, acquired, 10,000 miles away, in the white man's motherfucking war.

The fatality was an overweight Jewish kid from the Bronx, a basic trainee who had dropped out of a forced march. He had dropped out twice; the second time he couldn't get up. The NCO who brought him in, unconscious and red as a beet, wanted us to know what he thought of the caliber of soldier they were giving him these days.

"Couldn't march, couldn't run, couldn't keep up. All he could do was fuckin' eat. Now this. Where do I put him?"

Heat stroke.

We got his uniform off and filled a bathtub with ice cubes and lowered him in, one Gentile medic on each limb. He shit when he hit the ice and that was it, his final act as a soldier, his farewell address to Uncle Sam.

After Fort Polk we were given two weeks leave. I had a car, an orange-and-black Opel Kadett that my parents had given me for graduating from college. A Canadian woman and her daughter picked it up in California and drove it out to North Carolina. I drove it from North Carolina to Texas and then to Louisiana. Now Stu and I were driving it to Nashua, New Hampshire, where his parents and younger brother lived.

Nashua was a small university town, with old, well-kept buildings that would have been described as "quaint" in other parts of the country. It was mid-July but it felt like autumn compared to Texas and Louisiana. The leaves were beginning to turn. The fall semester would be starting soon. Stu had majored in Philosophy. A year older than I, he had been married, divorced, and then drafted. His wife had a funny-sounding name that I would remember if I ever heard it again. Stu never had a bad word to say about her. Like Wykes he never swore, never lost his temper, never lost his gentlemanly contempt for the military.

None of his old friends seemed to be around. One day we drove to the beach in Maine, my first look at the Atlantic Ocean: too cold and too rough to swim in. Canada was two states away, not a temptation for either of us. Soon we would be returning to Fort Bragg.

Stu's mother brought out the photo album. She showed me pictures of Stu when he was in high school, working on the roof with his father, on his knees with a hammer. Stu was good with his hands, she told me. They were doctor's hands, I told her. The astronauts were about to land on the moon. We watched it in their living room, the first American to hit a golf ball in outer space.

CHAPTER 24:

EVERYBODY BUT STU AND ME

Back at the fort, the hardest part of our training behind us, everybody who was going to get kicked out had been kicked out, everybody but Stu and me. We were the only trainees in the brigade who didn't think the ration of shit they were feeding us was fit for human consumption. Wykes, my only other friend in the Army, was in the stockade. With only a few weeks left until the orals exam and graduation, we had to make a career decision. Either we would graduate and become Green Berets and former Green Berets for the rest of our lives, or get out now before it was too late.

We decided to write the company commander a letter, advising him of our intentions and outlining some of our grievances.

The next morning we were ordered to report.

We had a new CO and a new first sergeant, First Sergeant De Luca (Sebastian E.) and Captain Donald Cappelletti having been reassigned while we were gone. Cappelletti had taken over the company after a tour in Vietnam and was getting out of the Army. Stu and I were both glad we didn't have to face De Luca. He was the kind of first sergeant you didn't want to disappoint. He and Cappelletti had run the company like a father-son team, with De Luca as the father. ("Call me 'Top.'") He was killed a year later in Laos, presumably by the enemy. He had plenty of them, including the sergeant major.

Our first meeting with the new CO didn't last very long. Stu and I both got the impression that he had come up through the ranks, meaning he had gone to Vietnam an NCO and come back an officer, not unusual during wartime. We could have been wrong about the battlefield commission—he could have gone to West Point for all we knew—but he came across like an NCO.

He turned out to be mildly pissed as opposed to highly pissed and gave us the military equivalent of a once-in-forever-in speech. There was no way we were getting out now, he told us, not after all the money they had spent on us. The figure he used was $300,000, as I recall, a lot of money in those days. Referring to it as "the taxpayers' money" and not wasting any of the taxpayers' time, he gave us the military cure-all for every human ailment. What we needed to do was get our silly heads out of our asses and get with the program and start taking some personal pride in what we were doing to become the best God-damned blah blah blahs in the blah blah blah, most of this directed at Golden, the Honor Graduate, whose head wasn't as far up his ass as mine was.

We took turns reminding him of the contents of our letter, offering him what we thought were compelling reasons for him to let us go. We might as well have been talking to the .50-caliber machine-gun brass that he kept on his desk, the empty shell casings that every lifer keeps his pencils in, or we could have been talking to the framed, autographed photo of our newly-installed Commander-in-Chief, Richard Milhous Nixon, hanging behind him on the wall, an image that Stu and I would have been throwing darts at if this had been a dart-throwing contest, but it wasn't, and we were abruptly saluted and dismissed.

The path of duty had been clearly defined for us. Our heads, no doubt, had been fully extricated.

One of the things you learn from these kinds of encounters, something that still sticks with me from my time in the military, is that it doesn't pay to overestimate your adversary. It was obvious that the Army was not remotely interested in anything that appeared reasonable or unreasonable to Stu and me as human beings, so why try to reason with them on that level?

I wanted to take the direct approach, in language that they could understand, which was right up my alley. I wanted to engage them in a battle of words since it was obvious that they could read even if they couldn't listen, and I could write even if I couldn't talk. Stu could talk. He used words like "dichotomy" and "juxtaposed." Between the two of us I didn't think there was anything they could do to stop us or dissuade us from our purpose. I was beginning to enjoy myself for the first time since leaving the fraternity house and wasn't about to start looking at all the little and not-so-little things the Army could do to make life even more miserable for us than it already was.

With characteristic caution Stu decided it would be better to let things die down a little before we threw anything new at them. No doubt this was the wiser, more mature approach, especially considering the way things turned out for the two of us. As Honor Graduate he had good reason to be cautious. He stood to lose a lot more than I did for one thing. The cadre liked him, the troops looked up to him, the doctors who had trained him had high hopes for him. All he had to do was stick it out a few more weeks and keep his mouth shut, and stay away from me, and he was sure to graduate *Summa Cum Laude* from Special Forces Medics. With his record he could count on a nice clean job in a hospital somewhere, possibly even Hawaii where the big medevac hospital was, promotion to E-4 at least, probably E-5 if he'd suck up to the right people. This would mean a substantial increase in his monthly allowance as well as a considerable boost to his social standing in the military: admission to the NCO Club and the NCO Mess Hall, decent housing, clean girls; but he wasn't interested, God bless him. For somebody with no religious background he had a lot of conviction.

The rest of our class, the guys we bunked with and jumped with and drank rotgut 3.2 American beer with, the only thing that seemed to matter to any of them was getting their dope and getting their "flashes," the long-awaited cloth insignia that would be awarded upon graduation, replacing the simple black metal pin-ons that marked us as trainees.

The dope they were getting from our laid-back platoon leader, Staff Sergeant Jim Slough (pronounced "Slaow"), a trainee like the rest of us but a lifer who lived off-post with his wife and kids. Slough's involvement in the dope-dealing gave it a homespun, fatherly touch, allowing the boys to be boys without having to sneak around off-post, possibly getting caught, thereby bringing dishonor to the brigade.

CHAPTER 25:

THE HONORABLE THING TO DO

One of the options that I wanted to consider, something that was sure to bring dishonor to the brigade, was the anti-war movement, then at its peak in the U.S. Stu had more of a conscience about the war than I did, so I thought this might be something that would appeal to him, but it didn't. He felt like a hypocrite, he said, being part of a unit that had gained its notoriety through stealth and mayhem—we both felt like hypocrites, masquerading as Green Berets when we were anything but—but using the anti-war movement for the express purpose of getting ourselves kicked *out* of the Green Berets would also not be the honorable thing to do, he felt, at least not for him. We may have gotten into some doctrinal disputation over this, I don't remember.

I didn't have any scruples about it one way or the other. The unbridled stupidity that ruled in our lives made it impossible for me to conceive of the Army fighting an intelligent war, much less a just war, so I never got around to looking at it from the ethical or moral point of view. Being treated like an idiot, that's what I considered to be immoral. Being forced to live with people who didn't mind being treated like animals, that's what made me want to kill.

That's what it was supposed to do, of course, what it was designed to do, what it almost always succeeds in doing, but in my case it backfired, thank the Lord. No credit to me. For whatever reason, I was never able to translate my hatred for the American way of death into some kind of useful, purposeful, "constructive" hatred for America's perceived enemies in Vietnam. There was no shortage of enemies in my life—I was surrounded by them—but they were all wearing the same uniform I was wearing. Or so I looked to me at the time.

Stu was right. I was more interested in lighting a fire under some macho military asses than I was in trying to stop the war. Nobody was going to stop it anyway, not by marching and demonstrating and singing "*Give Peace A Chance.*" There would be no end to the killing in Vietnam until the powers-that-be were God-damned good and ready to end it. I admired the civilians who were trying to talk some sense into their countrymen—they were doing something that I couldn't do—but trying to get the Army, the Navy, the Marines, the Air Force, the defense contractors, the arms manufacturers, the Church, the Pentagon, and their front-men, the politicians, to withdraw peacefully from Vietnam made as much sense to me as trying to get a school of sharks to turn vegetarian. First you kill the sharks, then you turn them into fertilizer for the vegetables.

So the peace routine, although it left something to be desired from a tactical point of view, was convenient. It was already up and running, even within the military, and it was something the lifers hated almost more than anything. It was a way to provoke the lifers that I found very appealing. It wasn't exactly tried-and-proven—I don't think anybody from the Green Berets had ever tried it before—but that made it even more appealing, a golden opportunity that I intended to take full advantage of, with or without Golden.

CHAPTER 26:

BRAGG BRIEFS HITS THE FAN

Shortly after our first run-in with the captain, I got wind of a group called "GIs United," short for "GIs United Against the War in Vietnam." I think Stu was the one who told me about them. I found out where they were holding their meetings and showed up one night.. They turned out to be ordinary soldiers, all of them draftees, all of them bored with their lot in the military or threatened by it—none of them wanted to go to Vietnam—and some with their own agenda.

I met the two leaders, one of them a David Somebody. He had a German-sounding name like Kauffmann or Kuhlmann, Jewish as could be. They called him "Rat." An energetic, inquisitive fellow with a nervous squint behind his glasses that was also ratlike, the name seemed to fit him. Rat's lieutenant was a lanky blonde Presbyterian from Minnesota who flashed the peace sign like it was going out of style. Which it was. Government treatment of the anti-war demonstrators had grown increasingly harsh by this time (late '69). Not many white college kids or peace-loving hippies wanted to get hit over the head or gassed more than once, much less shot at.

The Black Power Movement, on the other hand, the other side of the movement, the other side of the tracks, having grown up less delicately than the whites, was used to the sound of gunfire in their own neighbor-hoods and received correspondingly harsher treatment from the government.

I saw Rat, the Jewish boy, one more time after I got out of the Army. I had joined the Family by this time and was visiting my parents in Saratoga, California, sitting in the living room with my father, listening to a business program hosted by Myron Kandel. My mother was in the kitchen cooking dinner with the door closed because Myron's nasally voice bothered her.

I forget what she had on the stove that evening—she was a wonderful cook—but one of Myron's guests that afternoon, now an economist sitting on a government panel, wearing a black suit and a new pair of glasses, was none other than…you guessed it.

"Yo, Rat! Peace!"

He may have been working for the government back in 1969 for all I knew—nothing would surprise me about those days—but he was happy to have me that evening, especially when he found out I had a BA in Journalism. He wanted to start up a newspaper and needed an editor, somebody who could spell and punctuate, which again was right up my alley.

I ended up writing most of the first issue, including an interview with former Special Forces trainee Paul Wykes, who had been in and out of the stockade and had some stories to tell. Since I knew how to type, I ended up doing most of the "layout" for this first issue, on a stencil. I had the feeling there wasn't going to be a second issue, and with nobody telling me what to do, no managing editor looking over my shoulder, urging me to show restraint, I figured it was up to me to make sure that the right people would be aware of my involvement in this venture.

Bragg Briefs Number One hit the stands with everybody's name, rank, service number and unit posted under the masthead, plastered across the front page in red ink.

The ink wasn't my idea. One of Rat's contacts, a fellow who ran a print shop in Fayetteville, wanted to do the printing for us for free, but he had run out of black ink, so we decided to let him go with the red.

 Military Intelligence by this time, predictable as ever, was on our trail. The war to stop the spread of Communism in Southeast Asia was being waged just as assiduously—and just as intelligently—on the home front.

A notice appeared on the "A" Company bulletin board advising All Personnel to be on the lookout for a small but well-organized group of GIs whose stated goal was to undermine troop morale at this critical juncture in the war effort. (Nixon was getting ready to bomb Cambodia.) Any suspicious gatherings were to be reported immediately to the Company Commander. An ongoing investigation by MI had confirmed that these individuals, who called themselves "GIs United," were, if not under the direct employ of the government of Hanoi, certainly their willing dupes.

So the ink turned out to be a nice political touch.

CHAPTER 27:

SHEEP WITHOUT A SHEPHERD

The accusation that we were being used by the Communists may or may not have had some basis in fact. I wasn't with the movement long enough to prove it one way or the other—they sent me to Vietnam before I could get too deeply involved—but one incident in particular led me to suspect that Communist ideology, if not openly promoted within the anti-war community, was certainly tolerated by it.

In November, 1969 an estimated half a million Americans, including me, converged on Washington, D. C. for what was billed as the biggest anti-war gathering in the nation's history.

"The March on Washington," they called it.

It was a bright clear morning in the nation's capital, and Senator Eugene McCarthy, the Democrat from Minnesota who had successfully challenged LBJ in the '68 primary election, gave a bright clear speech in Lafayette Park that made it clear why the not-so-bright Democrats didn't want him running for president. He was way too passionate about the war, way too precise, and way too uncompromising for the average American voter.

After nearly two years in the Army and another long year to go, I was under civilian patronage again. There were civilians everywhere, loud-talking civilians, civilians with bullhorns, civilian girls huddled arm-in-arm on the sidewalks, stamping their feet to keep warm, trying to retain some of the heat from McCarthy's talk. You could see the steam coming out of their mouths, their long lovely civilian hair bristling in the cold.

Sheep without a shepherd. (Matthew 9:36)

They put the GI contingent at the head of the parade. My face is probably still in somebody's FBI file somewhere. At a signal from one of the bullhorns we started down Pennsylvania Avenue towards the Washington Monument, followed by the civilians. The GIs were led by a bearded skinny guy wearing the male hippy uniform of the day: Army-issue boots and fatigue jacket. He may have been a soldier once himself because he was calling cadence.

"LEFT!.... LEFT!.... LEFT, LEFT, LEFT!..."

I had enjoyed the senator's speech and was looking forward to the singing at the obelisk—Arlo Guthrie was waiting for us with his 12-string—but I didn't like being used by these people, whoever they were, and I didn't like marching on my day off. My FBI file would show me dropping out after a block or two and joining the throng on the sidewalk.

Whether these events were inspired or orchestrated or even infiltrated by the Communists, I had no way of knowing. I had read my share of Marx, Engels and Feuerbach by this time, enough to be able to recognize any overt Communist propaganda if I had seen it or heard it, but anything that wasn't overtly pro-American in those days was considered to be pro-Communist by the people who believed what Johnson and Nixon were telling them.

"My fellow Amurricans," LBJ called us, pronouncing it the way my Italian father did.

Nixon, the California boy who succeeded LBJ in the White House, had his own pet name for the people, referring to them solemnly in his speeches as the "Silent Majority." Later somebody would call them the "Moral Majority." They were silent all right—and they were moral as Hell—as long as you were one of them. If you were not one of them, and if you had no intention of ever becoming one of them, then they became noisy as Hell and mean as Hell.

My last encounter with these, my fellow Amurricans, was the day I left for Vietnam. Two busloads of them showed up at Clark Air Force Base to wish us godspeed as we went off to do battle with their enemies 10,000 miles away. There were 240 of us on the plane and maybe half that many civilians out there lining the runway, waving at us from behind a chain-link fence.

The women had their handkerchiefs out and their trusty flags. You could see their lips moving. The men were waving too, some with their fists, wishing us many one-shot kills and as few returning body bags and stretcher cases as possible, God willing. Some inside in the plane were waving back.

As we taxied down the runway (this was February, 1970), headed for Cam Ranh Bay and points beyond, the buses that had brought our civilian well-wishers to the airfield came into view, parked front-to-back behind the same fence. From the front of the first bus to the back of the second a white banner had been hung. If these buses were Greyhounds the banner would have been about 80 feet long and maybe 10 feet high. Painted down the length of it six-foot-high capital letters was the salutation, "AMERICA! LOVE IT OR LEAVE IT!"

We were leaving it all right. I couldn't get off the ground fast enough. Anything was better than another long year in the stateside Army, even if it meant getting shot at by people who thought I was their enemy.

Getting shot at by people who thought I was their enemy didn't bother me as much as being part of an invasion force that had never fought a war in its own backyard. From the Revolutionary War to the wars against the Indians and the Mexican to the war against the South, to the wars against the Germans and the Italians and the Japanese and the Koreans, every one of America's wars was fought in somebody else's backyard.

Now we were going against the Communists, who had fought plenty of wars in their own backyard. Like black America, they were used to the sound of gunfire in their own neighborhoods. They were better students of history than we were, too. Both the Russians and the Chinese had seen the rise and fall of empires in their own vast homelands: the Crimes for which history always exacts a Punishment.

More to the point, the followers of Marx, Mao and Ho Chi Minh were taking a Hell of a lot more casualties than we were. For every one of "our boys" being killed or wounded in Vietnam, tens of thousands of *their* boys, North and South Vietnamese, Cambodian and Laotian men, women, and children, husbands and wives, sons and daughters, brothers and sisters, grandfathers, grandmothers, farmers, doctors, poets, were losing not only their lives and limbs but their homes and villages as well. At least the Americans had something to come back to.★

How the leader of any nation with an ounce of compassion for his own people (as much compassion, say, as Johnson or Nixon had for their own people) would not do anything in his power to subvert the youth of an enemy nation, in this case America, before the leaders of that nation could put guns in their hands, was beyond me. The Americans would have done the same thing given the same opportunity.—If they had been smart enough.

A big "if."

If they had been really smart, as professing Christians, they would have been subverting Communist youth with the Gospel of Jesus Christ!— and saving themselves and the rest of the world all that heartache and bloodshed; and saving themselves from the wrath to come. (Matthew 3: 7; Luke 3: 7)

★The Vietnamese government estimates that three to five *million* of her citizens, the vast majority of them noncombatants, were killed during the American War alone; not to mention the half a million, give or take a few hundred thousand, who died during the American-backed French War.

CHAPTER 28:

THE CHAMP VERSUS THE CHUMPS

Where was the Christian Church while all this was going on? Where were the spokesmen for the Lamb of God and the Prince of Peace while the "Communist wolves" were ravaging the flock? The sad fact of the matter, until Dad came along and drafted us completely *out* of the God-damned System, there was no uncompromised Christian voice in America. With rare and feeble exceptions they were all bending over backwards, Catholics and Protestants alike, doing their damnedest to give Johnson and Nixon and their ilk the benefit of the doubt, paying homage to a System that was becoming more anti-Christ by the minute! Blessing the troops! Biting their tongues! They're still doing it.

The only prominent American I knew of during that era who dared to lift up his voice against the murderous American war machine wasn't even a Christian! While dear Billy Graham, "America's foremost spiritual spokesman," was hobnobbing with two of the most heartless crooks in the history of American politics, a newly-converted black Muslim prize-fighter was taking it on the chin for saying what any Christian worth his salt should have been saying, what Jesus Himself surely would have said if

He could have gotten any of His professed followers to open their mouths.

He didn't have any trouble getting Muhammad Ali to open *his* mouth!—but then Ali was no patriot. What was left of Ali's patriotism must have disappeared with the hamburger that he wasn't allowed to eat in his hometown diner the day of his triumphal return from the Rome Olympics. When the Army came looking for him seven years later, Ali (formerly Cassius Clay), now the heavyweight champion of the world, could say with the apostle Peter (formerly Simon Bar-jona), "Whether it be right in the sight of God to hearken unto you more than unto God, judge ye!" (Acts 4:19)

He could call the Vietnamese brothers and sisters while his white Christian accusers, faithful sons of the Republic, could think of nothing better to call them but "gooks." The toughest man on the planet, arguably the greatest fighter in any weight class in the history of the sport, could refuse to take up arms against the poor and the downtrodden because he belonged to Allah the Compassionate and not to a nation of self-righteous bullies!

'"And the common people heard him gladly." (Mark 12:37)

Those who should have been his greatest allies, the first to rush to his defense in his hour of need—this pivotal moment in Muslim-Christian relations, this moment of supreme opportunity—were no doubt huddled in their churches, their Christless tombs, praying for his early demise, hoping he'd get bumped off like Malcolm X did.

They underestimated Muhammad Ali as a man of God as they had always underestimated him as a fighter. They took his title and his money and threatened to shut him up in prison for five years, but they couldn't get him to shut his mouth, and they couldn't get the millions of Muslims around the world who were praying for him, beseeching Allah to vindicate His servant, to shut *their* mouths.

And the Lord did it! The Louisville Lip, the butterfly who stung like a bee, "The onliest poet laureate in boxin' history!"—took everything that Uncle Sam could throw at him. They had him on the ropes for three and a half merciless years, and it cost him everything, everything that matters to a fighter: his title, his money, his youth, his marvelous physical gifts. White Christian America robbed Muhammad Ali of everything but his indomitable spirit and his unquenchable sense of humor.

And he came back after four years and whupped Foreman! That's probably what he'll be remembered for, the night in Zaire when Foreman bit the dust and the clouds wept for joy, but I'll always remember Muhammad Ali for the tap dance he did on Uncle Sam's proud white head.

CHAPTER 29:

REGULAR PROGRAMMING

News travels fast in the military. The morning after *Bragg Briefs* hit the fan, the company clerk came to get me, happy to announce that I was in deep shit. (The prepositional phrase "in trouble" doesn't exist in military syntax.) The CO was waiting for me, he said. The CO was pissed—highly pissed. He, the company clerk, had never seen him so pissed.

Sure enough, a copy of *Bragg Briefs* lay open on the captain's desk as I was ushered in that morning. I could tell he'd been reading it. His face was the same color as the ink. Without a word and without returning my salute, he took his hand and sent my eight pages of hard work sailing to the floor, letting me know that I had messed with the wrong man. I was a little pissed myself. I was about to get raked over the coals by somebody who hadn't been the least bit interested in anything that Stu or I had tried to say to him privately, in this same office; now he was all bent out of shape because I had gone public with it.

This what I hated about the damned Army, what I still hate about it every time I have to listen to it. Every time I turn the TV on to watch the news and find out that "regular programming" has about to be pre-empted by latest war; every time one of these well-decorated turkeys (what's known in the journalism racket as a "military spokesperson") gets up in front of the cameras, clears his throat, and commences his assault on the English language, I'm back in the Army again, listening to the same old bullshit that brought us Vietnam.

Nothing has changed in 30-some years, least of all the ladies and gentlemen of the press, without whom none of this well-orchestrated bullshit would be possible. They're still letting him get away with it, not because they're ladies or gentlemen, either, or because there's anything in their job description that says they have to sit there with their heads up their asses, their lips carefully sealed, waiting for the misery to end so they can collect their free drinks.

The victims of this sordid breach of the public trust, meanwhile, the poor suckers who foot the bill for every bite of food the soldier eats, every bed he sleeps in, every bomb he drops, every bullet he fires, every drop of blood he spills, every drop of Jack Daniels, will never get their money's worth until they sign up for it like I did. Because signing up for it—relinquishing your rights as a civilian while accepting, under oath, the duties and responsibilities of a soldier—is the only known bridge between the two worlds, the only way to get across the gulf that separates the taxpayer from the tax-exempt.

It's the only way to get across legally. Presumably there should be some way for any civilian with enough nerve and enough imagination—even a lady or gentleman of the press with little nerve and no imagination—to find his or her way onto military property; but even if he or she were able to get inside, and even if he or she were able to get somebody on the inside to open up, it would still be soldiers talking to civilians. It still wouldn't be the real thing because the real thing has nothing to do with spilling the beans about the military. The real thing is letting the military spill its own beans, something it is eminently capable of doing, something it has long been in the habit of doing, without the help and of course without the knowledge of the taxpayer.

This miniscule minority, estimated to be less than 1% of the population, knows what kind of beans I'm talking about.

CHAPTER 30:

DEATH IN THE AFTERNOON

Off-camera we find the military man in his own element, amongst his own kin, or near-kin. In the company of other military mouths, even those who are far beneath him in the pecking order—and I was as far down as you could get—a well-lubricated military spokesperson will shoot his mouth off about things that few civilians would dare to discuss openly with anybody but a psychiatrist and a team of lawyers.

For example—and this is something that anybody from my generation should be able to relate to—until I got to Fort Bragg and became privy to the discussions that some of the lifers loved to entertain themselves with before dismissing us for evening chow, it had never occurred to me that anybody but a psychopath would be interested in the assassination of the 35th President of the United States from a *ballistics* point of view.

Those of you who have never handled guns or seen what a fast-moving projectile can do to animal and human flesh might be interested in a couple definitions here. (From The Oxford American Dictionary):

1. *Triangulation*: to divide into triangles. to measure or map out an area in surveying by means of calculations based on a network of triangles.

2. *Trajectory*: the path of a bullet or rocket etc. or of a body moving under certain forces.

Triangulation and a flat trajectory: that was the ticket, boys and girls. A flat-shooting varmint rifle—a .222 Hornet, say, with hollow points—that's what you needed to bring down a presidential pants-man.

"Hell, an M-16 would be better than that silly elephant gun that Oswald used! Man, what a way to screw up a good piece of lead!"

If they had done the job right, according to the loose cannons from "A" Company, if they had used the right people with the right equipment and the right kind of *experience*—you could hear SFC D. Smith clearing his throat at the suggestion—the cleanup crew at Dealey Plaza wouldn't have been able to *find* JFK's head.

Giggle giggle.

But the minute anybody tries to help them get their message across, so the rest of the world can benefit from their expertise—their *savoir-faire* and their *joie de vivre*—they act like you're betraying some sacred trust, trampling on the graves of all the brave men and women who had blah blah blah'd for the blah blah blah.

I was, in the words of the captain, a disgrace to my country, a disgrace to the uniform, and a disgrace to the beret I wore. That was the good news. The bad news was that there was nothing he could do about it. He couldn't take me out behind the motor pool and have me shot, for one thing, which is what he wanted to do, what he would have done if this had been the good old days, back when America's enemies got what they deserved, when soldiers were soldiers and traitors were lined up in front of a firing squad. He couldn't even kick my sorry ass out of the Green Berets!—because the Constitution that I had disgraced gave me the right to express my views as I saw fit, as long as I did it off-post and not during duty hours.

Diss-missed. No salute and no walking papers.

Here again I had overestimated my adversary, still thinking like a college boy. I had just trampled on his most sacred beliefs—his duty as a soldier, his pride as a patriot, his hat—and I had done it in broad daylight! I had done everything but challenge him to a duel!

But I hadn't broken any *regulations* yet.

That's the Army for you, that's the way they operate. They say it's different in the other branches of the service—I wouldn't know—but in the Army anything goes. You can *be* anything in the Army, just like it says on the recruiting poster. You can be a white supremacist, a black supremacist, a drunk, a wife-beater, a drug addict, a mass murderer, a raving Sodomite—you can even be a no-good disloyal sonofabitch like I was!—but as long as you do your job for Uncle Sam, the Army will generally turn a blind eye to your imperfections, especially if your imperfections are the kind that *complement* your job for Uncle Sam.

A mean streak, for example. That's one little behavioral quirk they won't hassle you for unless it spreads too far and the civilian press gets hold of it, like it did after the My Lai massacre, when meanness spread like wildfire and a village full of unarmed old men, women, children and infants were herded into a drainage ditch and pot-shot, gang-raped, Sodomized and fed to the flies.

Meanness—and all the petty little shibboleths that go along with it— is the lifeblood of the military. It's what happens to people who give themselves to an institution that confers on them the right to kill, and then justifies it for them by telling them it's the *enemy* they're killing.

Who's the enemy? Ask the president. Better yet, ask the chaplain.

Once you acquiesce in this little drama—and every soldier comes to terms with it sooner or later, one way or the other—once you let somebody tell you that you owe it to your country to play God with your fellow man; especially once you've pulled the trigger a few times and seen what a mess it makes; then I don't see how you can have much of a conscience about anything else.

These guys who beat their wives, for example, a common occurrence in the military.

"Hey, man, I didn't kill her, did I? I didn't cut her ears off and send'm to her brother in Pennsylvania! I smacked her around a little bit! So what? She's my old lady! She had it coming! While I was over there plugging gooks and getting a bad rep, she was back home plugging the major and living high on the hog!

"And these damned civilians! What are *they* complaining about? I'm over there doing their job! And they're *paying* me for it!"

CHAPTER 31:

MY MOTHER AND MY BRETHREN

Compare this, if you will, with life in the Family. Compare the standard of discipline and loyalty that I've just described for you, in one of the toughest, hardest-to-get-into, hardest-to-get-out-of outfits in the military, with the standard that you're expected to uphold as a member of the Lord's Army.

Some of you don't like this characterization; I know that. Some of you wonder whether the U. S. military precepts that Dad and Maria and Peter have invoked down through the years even apply in any real sense to life in the Family today. I can't tell you whether they do or not.

"Let every man be fully persuaded in his own mind." (Romans 14: 5)

But I can tell you that they applied 15 or 20 years ago when we were still an army. They applied in back in 1974 when I joined the outfit known as the Children of God. The uniform didn't amount to much but the lifestyle made the Green Berets look like the Girl Scouts!

I didn't know what discipline *was* until I joined the Family. Much less did I know anything about devotion to duty or self-sacrifice or laying down my life for my friends. I didn't have any friends. I do now. Three years ago I found out who my friends were. After a lifetime of virtually uninterrupted good health, I woke up one morning to find blood on my sheets: stage IV melanoma.

I was living in a busy office unit at the time, new to the home, far from being indispensable to the work. Instead of sending me back to my previous home or back to the States for treatment, which would have been the logical, medically-expedient thing to do, I was taken off the schedule and given time to read and pray and seek the Lord about the "little dog line" of His will.★ In the afternoons I was free to go on bike rides and hikes into the countryside while others took my place on the schedule.

Those of you who don't like to fish can skip the next few pages. If you think fishing is a waste of time, you're probably in good company. Dad himself, the one time I can remember him talking about it, reckoned it was foolishness; at least it was to him as a serious-minded youth. In later years he did confess that sitting in a boat on a lonely lake somewhere might be a good way to get away from your wife, but I think he was just giving other men the benefit of the benefit of the doubt.

Looking back on my own youthful pursuits, I have to admit that I might have been better off chasing girls like Dad did, or chasing a career like my father did, but fishing was what I was good at, along with hunting and going to school and going to church.

When I joined the Family I had to forsake my love for the out-of-doors, my lifelong habit of participating in the out-of-doors with a gun and a fishing pole. We were encouraged to go on bike rides and nature walks, sightseeing trips with the kids etc.—all these were considered to be *kosher*, edifying ways of getting a little fresh air and exercise, even a way to better oneself culturally—but my heart was never in it.

Occasionally, as opportunity presented itself (The Lord was always "casting our lines in pleasant places," especially in the Germanic countries where "the nature," as they call it, is very diligently preserved by God and the Germans.), I would fall happily into temptation, but I never had a peace about it. At least now I knew what to call it. (Romans 14: 23)

If it wasn't for the cancer I would probably still be sneaking around. I also have Angela to thank. She was never one to encourage me to go fishing unless it was to get rid of me for a few hours—it works both ways—but now that my health had taken a nosedive, she had become my fulltime cook and dietician, managing my lunches and dinners with the same diligence and attention to detail with which she managed my side of the bedroom.

Of particular concern to her was the chicken we were getting in the provisioning, our main source of protein at the time. It was slathered with all manner of guck and gunk, already cooked when we got it. It tasted good and you could live on it if you had to—everybody else was living on it—but not if you were dying of cancer.

I wasn't exactly dying, by the way—I'm still not dead yet—but the prognosis for stage IV, malignant, metastasized melanoma was pretty grim. I went on the internet one night to see what it had to say about Stage IV. Stage V, it said, was "Deceased."

Lamb and veal were available locally, but expensive. Store-bought fish were also available, also expensive, and that's where I drew the line. We were living in a country that was crawling with trout—crawling with laws too. We lived at the foot of a mountain. Behind us was a lake, also full of fish, and full of tourists. Following the main road around the lake in either direction, every few kilometers or so you would come to a lovely little stream filled with lovely little *forellen*. You could see them down there from the bridges, scooting for cover, fresh lively protein, probably the only clean protein left on the planet, along with some of our feathered and furry friends, none of whom had been a regular part of my diet in a good many years, sad to say.

Following the main road from our house, heading northeast, you came to the village of Altdorf, with the statue of Wilhelm Tell is in the middle of the square, protective arm around his son, crossbow at the ready. Following the same road maybe a kilometer or two outside of town, you came to a stream that passed under the road on its way to the lake. Just before the stream was a narrow paved road that led uphill to the left and then veered off to the right past some houses, stopping at a fence, where I would park the bike.

Maybe 75 meters down the hill past this fence was my own private fishing grounds. In the two or three months that I frequented this place I never saw another human being or a beer can or a cigarette butt or a candy wrapper or any sign telling me I wasn't supposed to be there.

The stream was in good shape, running a little high this time of year, but clear and cold and lovely to drink, "the boids were choipin,"★★ and the little hills rejoiced on every side. (Psalm 65: 12)

If you've ever approached *salmo trutta* in a setting like this, water plunging down the mountain, racing through the meadows, past the ferns and the beeches and the firs and the alders, spilling over the boulders, slowing down a little here and there, maybe five meters across at the widest, a meter deep at the deepest, full of wild browns that had never seen a worm with a hook in it, you'll understand why I was itching to get my dietary plan ratified by the home's leadership.

Besides scouting out the local possibilities I was doing a lot of reading, including Kristen's "Fight For Life!" which became a mainstay over the next few months, along with David Livingstone's *Missionary Travels and Researches*, which I happened to come across on the internet one evening, my dear mother having bought us our first computer, a 10-pounder.

It's a long file that begins with Livingstone's boyhood in Scotland. This was a year or two before Angela or I had any idea of going to South Africa, by the way. I was finding, to my great delight, that I had something in common with the legendary Scotsman besides the fact that we were both Protestants.

Here was a guy who went to the ends of the earth to spread the gospel, suffering every deprivation imaginable, forsaking his wife and kids, losing his health, getting mauled by a lion; a man who, perhaps more than any Christian since the apostle Paul, exemplifies what a disciple should be willing to do for the love of Christ, in just plain thanks for His salvation; a man whose head you might expect to be perpetually in the clouds, never to utter a word that wasn't deeply, steadfastly religious; yet he comes across in his writings as a very down-to-earth fellow indeed.

He did more hunting than fishing in Africa—an eland or a buffalo feeds a lot more people than a fish does—but he tells of an incident in his boyhood in Scotland on the River Clyde, near the family residence in Blantyre, when he or one of his brothers ties into a salmon. He doesn't say much about the fish, how big it was or the exact species, or even the kind of tackle they were using, but I suspect, from reading the narrative, that they were hand-lining.

Hand-lining, as you may know, is a respectable, dependable, unobtrusive way to catch most fish, including trout. It wouldn't be an easy way to land a fish as quick and powerful as a salmon, but certainly possible if you knew what you were doing and took your time. I have never caught a salmon but I have caught steelhead and some fairly hefty browns and rainbows, and I think I know what the Livingstone boys were thinking that day on the River Clyde, and it wasn't "catch-and-release."

★★★

They get the fish in after an exciting tussle. David, the eldest, drops to one knee, genuflecting, as it were, before this noble creature, arguably the king of all gamefish, about to become the best-eating of all gamefish. With his left hand he takes it under the belly, giving thanks. Right-handed, he delivers it to the priest. (A priest is a tool, a blunt instrument, a small bludgeon used for hitting fish over the head. The word "priest" comes from the notion of administering last rites to the fish.)

Charles, the youngest, loosens his belt. Not wanting to stumble the local townsfolk, David, the future missionary to southern Africa, takes the glistening, still-quivering fish by the base of the tail and slides it headfirst down the leg of Charles' trousers. Charlie tightens his belt, pulls his shirt down and off they go, whistling a hymn, passing through the neighboring villages on their way home, "causing passersby to comment sympathetically on the poor lad with the limp and the swollen leg."

Writing about this adventure years later, Livingstone makes the following observation. I don't have it in front of me but this is the gist of it.

"*I don't believe that God would put these fish in the rivers just for rich people to catch.*"

I let out a whoop when I read this! This was the answer to my prayer! in the words of a man that no sane Christian would dare to gainsay or resist. This was the "word of faith" that I had been earnestly beseeching God for. I was on the right track!

"If he ask a fish, will He give him a serpent?" (Matthew 7: 10)

I didn't get healed because I went fishing. I got healed because Jesus took a whipping for my sake and because I had enough sense not to listen to the Devil. I said no to the Devil. God did the rest. Fishing was an afterthought, but the Lord used it, knowing my frame. Fishing—specifically trout fishing—became the one thing I could do that would absolutely get my mind off the cancer and the voice of cancer. (*"That little twinge in your back there that you never felt before? That's the cancer kicking in, sucker!"*)

From the moment I left the manure pile in the backyard, climbed on my bike and headed down the road with my supply of worms for the day, Mother Nature pulling me to her bosom, to the time I got back in the saddle, wet to the waist and happy as a cormorant, I never had a thought of the two lab reports telling me that my days were numbered.

I got healed when a brother named Tim, visiting from England about a month after I was diagnosed, greeted me in the foyer with the following news:

"Wow, Phil, what a miracle! Totally healed of cancer!"

It was news to me, Brother!

I got healed when Dr. Zisiadis, the Greek dermatologist, a determined unbeliever who performed the excavation on my back, put his arm around me at the end of each visit and say, in *Suisse Deutsch*, "God must really love you!"

I got healed when Dr. Eberle, the surgeon who removed the lymph node from under my left arm, apologized for not being able to do it sooner. Heidi and I went to see him on a Saturday. Sitting with us in his office, looking through my records, he told us that the lymph node, obviously necrotic, was doing God knows what to the rest of my lymphatic system and had to come out right away. But it was too late to do it today. Arrangements had to be made with the operating theatre and the anesthetist etc. And tomorrow was Sunday, his day off, his only day to spend time with his son.

He, the surgeon, who was doing the procedure *gratis*, as well as supplying his own anesthetist and his own pathologist, was asking me, the patient, if it was OK if we waited until Monday morning!

When God puts people like this in your path, it's not hard to believe that you're in good hands.

I got healed when Heidi Helfenschwil, the sister who provisioned every slice of medical treatment that I received over a period of about four months, including Dr. and Mrs. Zisiadis, Dr. Eberle the surgeon, and the oncologist, whose name I can't remember; called to me one afternoon as I was heading down the stairs to get the car ready for a trip to the hospital in St. Gallen.

"Philip! There's a message for you from Maria!"

Wishing me well and letting me know that she and the folks in her home were praying for me, she ended her note with a Keys Promise.

"*The keys of healing, relief and rejuvenation await your command. At the call of your prayers I will activate these keys on your behalf. They will bring strength, comfort and physical renewal to your bodies. They will restore health to your flesh. They will work healing miracles for you.*" (Matthew 16: 19)

I memorized this on the way to the hospital and Heidi and Angela and I claimed it together before we went in.

I was about to get my first PET scan (Positron Emission Tomography), to see whether and how far the cancer had spread. Dr. Nordstrom, the young Norwegian radiologist, took me to the room that the PET Scan machine was parked in, a large, imposing, cream-colored machine, maybe two and a half meters high and three meters long, in appearance not unlike the sliding table saws that are common in Europe.

I lay on my back on the table, a narrow bed that ran on tracks into a closed, brightly-lit chamber. Dr. Nordstrom pushed some buttons and I slid in headfirst towards the "blade." A few seconds later he pushed another button and I slid back out, for better or for worse, my positrons having been thoroughly emissioned. This procedure, lasting only a few seconds, was supposed to be 98% effective in determining cancer metastasis.

Dr. Nordstrom went to the lab to see what the computer had to say and I joined Angela and Heidi in the lobby. A few minutes later he came striding down the hallway towards us, holding a piece of paper in front of him, a pleased medical smile on his face. I was clean, according to the cancer-detecting machine

I got healed, finally, when Hebrews 10: 38 came to me out of nowhere. I had heard and read this verse many times, but always in relation to faith and justice. Now it was talking about *living*.

"The just shall *live* by faith" is the way it came to me, with emphasis on the verb "live."

> live1 (liv) lived, liv´ing, vi.
>
> 1 to be alive; have life
> 2 a) to remain alive b) to last; endure
> 3 a) to pass one's life in a specified manner [to live happily] b) to regulate or conduct one's life [to live by a strict moral code]
> 4 to enjoy a full and varied life [to really know how to live]
> 5 a) to maintain life; support oneself [to live on a pension] b) to be dependent for a living (with off)
> 6 to feed; subsist; have as one's usual food [to live on fruits and nuts]
> 7 to make one's dwelling; reside
> 8 to remain in human memory of [men's good deeds live after them]

This was the verse that converted Martin Luther and it converted what was left of my unbelief into the absolute certainty that I was going to live, and not die, at least not of the cancer.

I got healed because nobody tried to talk me out of it. Even Angela, who had better reason than anybody to doubt my medical judgment, after years of trying to get me to see a doctor about the mole on my back, which she could see and I couldn't, and now seeing me getting what I deserved, held her peace. Whatever doubts that she or others may have had about the narrow-minded approach that I was taking to the crisis that I had brought into their midst, they kept to themselves. Not even the doctors tried to talk me out of it.

The last one we went to was the oncologist. I was surprised to hear him tell us that our decision to forego further treatment made as much sense to him, medically, as what he was obliged to tell us as a physician. He told us what the dermatologist and the surgeon had already told us, that people who live in an atmosphere of faith—"a positive atmosphere," he called it—stand a better chance of surviving a deadly disease than those who live in a negative, fearful state.

His professional recommendation: the removal of another 13 or 14 lymph nodes from under my left arm and the re-excavation of my back. This tissue would then be sent to a pathologist, who would "slice it up like a cucumber"—his words—and then look at it under a microscope. If these pieces of my anatomy were found to be cancer-free, I could then be declared "clinically healed," as opposed to miraculously healed, but the procedure would have to be repeated every six months!

I looked over at Angela who was better at keeping a straight face than I was.

"So you remove another thirteen or fourteen lymph nodes from under my arm and take another chunk out of my back."

He nodded.

"And you send this to the pathologist, who slices it up like a cucumber and looks at it under a microscope."

Another nod.

"And if it's still good you put it back in again, right?"

This was as close to a smile as we got from the oncologist. It was time to go. He had told us what we needed to hear.

Passing through the train station on our way home, Angela bought me a double espresso with whipped cream and a cinnamon roll.

"*Now the just shall live by faith: but if any man draw back, my soul shall have no pleasure in him. But we are not of them who draw back unto perdition; but of them that believe to the saving of the soul.*" (Hebrews 10: 38, 39)

★"The Little Dog Dream," #535.

★★One of Dad's jokes. Two guys are sitting outdoors enjoying the weather.

"The boids are really choipin' today," the guy from New Jersey says.

The guy from California looks at him. "You mean chirping?"

"What?"

"Chirping. The birds are *chirping*, not choiping."

The guy from New Jersey looks at him and says, "Sounds like choipin' to me!"

★★★ "Catch-and-release" is the modern-day perversion that treats God's creation as a plaything, a way for man to demonstrate his superiority over nature ("I'm smarter than a fish!"), his magnanimity of spirit, his tackle, his wardrobe, and of course his camera equipment. Only the fish is playing for keeps.

CHAPTER 32:

MY HAT AND THE CAPTAIN'S HAT

On my way out the door I had an idea. The sob story about the hat—my hat and the captain's hat—reminded me of something that had happened back in jump school.

One day at Fort Benning I walked into the wrong barracks and wound up talking to some Marines. (Army, Navy SEALs, Marines, Air Force, along with some foreign personnel, took parachute training together at Fort Benning, Georgia.)

Next to where I was standing was one of their tightly-made bunks. Sitting precisely in the middle of this bunk was a hat, called a Marine Corps soft hat. It's a round-looking hat with a short bill, like an upside-down can of tuna with the lid sticking out. I hated wearing hats but this one looked softer and more comfortable than the stiff baseball hats we had to wear in the Army, so I asked if I could try it on.

I didn't know which of them was the owner of the hat, so my question was directed generally towards the assembled Marines, who stood facing me in a line, maybe four of them. They seemed friendly enough. We were all taking the same training together and we were all headed to the same jungle.

One of them said, "OK, go ahead."

Sure enough, it fit perfect. Assuming this fellow to be the owner of the hat, I asked him if he wanted to trade me for something.

Looking over at his buddies again and then down at my boots, he pointed and said, "What size?"

I told him.

A pair of size-12 Army-issue leather boots would suit him just fine, he said.

So I went and got the boots, which was a dumb thing to do. Not only was a pair of Army-issue leather boots worth a lot more than the hat, there was no way the Army was going to let me wear headgear belonging to an opposing branch of the military, especially not the Marines, whose adversarial relationship with the Army was legendary.

But I had a brand-new pair of Corcoran Jump Boots (pronounced *Cock-rins*) back at my barracks, dress boots that I had bought recently at the PX, so I had an extra pair of regular-issue boots that I didn't need anymore.

We had better boots than they did but they had better hats.

And I still had this hat! It was down in the bottom of my duffel bag, along with my civilian clothes and my illicit reading material.

Next morning (this was the day after getting raked over the coals by Captain What's-his-name) I joined the stampede in the stairwell for the last time, wearing my beret for the last time.

At the bottom of the stairs was a glass door that opened outward onto concrete steps. Here you took a left. My place in the formation was maybe 20 meters away, maybe a 10-second walk or a five-second run if I was in a hurry, which I wasn't. I had to time it just right. From the preparatory command ("Cum-pa-*NEE!*") to the final command ("Uh-tenn…*HUAH!*") I had two seconds to fall in next to Golden while getting my beret off and my Marine Corps soft hat out of my fatigue pants and onto my head.

Golden was already out there and didn't know what I was up to. He would be on my immediate left. Looking towards the front, where the cadre stood, our place in the formation was left field, rear squad, close to the right flank, as far from home plate as we could get. We figured if they couldn't see us they wouldn't be able to hear us either.

Today they were going to see me. They were going to hear from me, too.

"Cum-pa-*NEE!*"

As I took my place next to Golden, switching hats, I caught a chuckle out of my left ear. It would be the only chuckle I would get that day, the only one I needed.

"Uh-tenn...*HUAH!*"....

"SEM-PAIR *FEE!*"★ I hollered at the top of my lungs.

Maybe five seconds went by—Daniel in the lions' den with a can of fresh tuna on my head—before two bruisers grabbed me from behind, one on each arm, and hauled me across the grass and up the steps to the first sergeant's office.

Mission accomplished.

★"*Semper Fi!*" as you may know, is the Marine Corps motto, the abbreviated form of *Semper Fidelis*, Latin for "Always Faithful." It's a fine saying as sayings go but the Marines always mispronounce it. I don't know why. Latin is an easy language to pronounce unless you're Irish or English. The vowel sounds are all short: Ah, eh, ee, oh, oo.

As in the Christmas song, "*Adeste Fidelis.*" ("Ah-dess-tay Fee-day-lees.")

I didn't find this out about the Marines until afterwards. At the time I thought I was pronouncing it the same way they did, which is to say correctly.

Not to brag, but I might be the first jarhead in the history of the Corps to get it right.

End of Part I